ROUNDELAY

Five Linked Short Plays to Be Performed in
No Particular Order

by Alan Ayckbourn

samuelfrench.co.uk

FOR AMATEUR PRODUCTION ENQUIRIES

UNITED KINGDOM AND WORLD
EXCLUDING NORTH AMERICA
plays@samuelfrench.co.uk
020 7255 4302/01

Each title is subject to availability from Samuel French,
depending upon country of performance.

THINKING ABOUT PERFORMING A SHOW?

There are thousands of plays and musicals available to perform from Samuel French right now, and applying for a licence is easier and more affordable than you might think

From classic plays to brand new musicals, from monologues to epic dramas, there are shows for everyone.

Plays and musicals are protected by copyright law, so if you want to perform them, the first thing you'll need is a licence. This simple process helps support the playwright by ensuring they get paid for their work and means that you'll have the documents you need to stage the show in public.

Not all our shows are available to perform all the time, so it's important to check and apply for a licence before you start rehearsals or commit to doing the show.

LEARN MORE & FIND THOUSANDS OF SHOWS

Browse our full range of plays and musicals, and find out more about how to license a show
www.samuelfrench.co.uk/perform

Talk to the friendly experts in our Licensing team for advice on choosing a show and help with licensing
plays@samuelfrench.co.uk   020 7387 9373

Acting Editions

BORN TO PERFORM

Playscripts designed from the ground up to work the way you do in rehearsal, performance and study

---

Larger, clearer text for easier reading

Wider margins for notes

Performance features such as character and props lists, sound and lighting cues, and more

---

+ CHOOSE A SIZE AND STYLE TO SUIT YOU

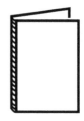

STANDARD EDITION

Our regular paperback book at our regular size

SPIRAL-BOUND EDITION

The same size as the Standard Edition, but with a sturdy, easy-to-fold, easy-to-hold spiral-bound spine

LARGE EDITION

A4 size and spiral bound, with larger text and a blank page for notes opposite every page of text – perfect for technical and directing use

LEARN MORE   **samuelfrench.co.uk/actingeditions**

Other plays by ALAN AYCKBOURN
published and licensed by Samuel French

Absent Friends

Arrivals and Departures

A Small Family Business

Awaking Beauty

Bedroom Farce

Body Language

Callisto 5

The Champion of Paribanou

A Chorus of Disapproval

Comic Potential

Communicating Doors

Confusions

A Cut in the Rates

Dreams from a Summer House

Drowning on Dry Land

Ernie's Incredible Illucinations

Man of the Moment

Mixed Doubles

Mr. A's Amazing Maze Plays

Mr Whatnot

My Very Own Story

My Wonderful Day

Neighbourhood Watch

The Norman Conquests: Table Manners; Living Together;
Round and Round the Garden

Private Fears in Public Places

Relatively Speaking

The Revengers' Comedies

RolePlay

Season's Greetings

Sisterly Feelings

Snake in the Grass

Suburban Strains

Sugar Daddies

Taking Steps

Ten Times Table

Things We Do for Love

**Other plays by ALAN AYCKBOURN
licensed by Samuel French**

ABOUT THE AUTHOR

Alan Ayckbourn has worked in theatre as a playwright and director for over fifty years, rarely if ever tempted by television or film, which perhaps explains why he continues to be so prolific. To date he has written more than eighty plays, many one act plays and a large amount of work for the younger audience. His work has been translated into over thirty-five languages, is performed on stage and television throughout the world and has won countless awards.

Major successes include: *Relatively Speaking, How the Other Half Loves, Absurd Person Singular, Bedroom Farce, A Chorus of Disapproval,* and *The Norman Conquests.* In recent years, there have been revivals of *Season's Greetings* and *A Small Family Business* at the National Theatre; in the West End *Absent Friends, A Chorus of Disapproval, Relatively Speaking* and *How the Other Half Loves*; and at Chichester Festival Theatre, major revivals of *Way Upstream* in 2015, and *The Norman Conquests* in 2017.

Artistic Director of the Stephen Joseph theatre from 1972–2009, where almost all his plays have been first staged, he continues to direct his latest new work there. He has been inducted into American Theater's Hall of Fame, received the 2010 Critics' Circle Award for Services to the Arts and became the first British playwright to receive both Olivier and Tony Special Lifetime Achievement Awards. He was knighted in 1997 for services to the theatre.

AUTHOR'S NOTE

Roundelay consists of five short, self-contained plays, written to be played in any sequence.

There are therefore (apparently!) 120 possibilities as to the order in which they could be performed.

Many are connected, sometimes through shared characters, sometimes through overlapping narrative.

Some are prequels to others, being themselves in turn sequels to others.

It is hoped that during a run they will be played in as many different orders as there are performances, employing simple staging to allow minimal gaps between each scene.

Ideally, there should be a single interval after the first three plays, whichever those may be.

MUSIC USE NOTE

Licensees are solely responsible for obtaining formal written permission from copyright owners to use copyrighted music in the performance of this play and are strongly cautioned to do so. If no such permission is obtained by the licensee, then the licensee must use only original music that the licensee owns and controls. Licensees are solely responsible and liable for all music clearances and shall indemnify the copyright owners of the play(s) and their licensing agent, Samuel French, against any costs, expenses, losses and liabilities arising from the use of music by licensees. Please contact the appropriate music licensing authority in your territory for the rights to any incidental music.

IMPORTANT BILLING AND CREDIT REQUIREMENTS

If you have obtained performance rights to this title, please refer to your licensing agreement for important billing and credit requirements.

FIRST PERFORMANCE INFO

ROUNDELAY

Roundelay consists of five one-act plays: The Agent,
The Judge, The Novelist, The Politician and The Star.

First performance at Stephen Joseph Theatre, Scarborough:
Round auditorium on 9 September 2014.

Tour premiere: 21 January 2015
at the Yvonne Arnaud Theatre, Guildford
Staging: End-stage

With the following cast:

Tom	RUSSELL DIXON
Blanche/Mrs Miller	ALEXANDRA MATHIE
Roz	KRYSTLE HILTON
Lindy Kuze/Mrs Kuyper	BROOKE KINSELLA
Russ	RICHARD STACEY
Lance/Sean	LEIGH SYMONDS
Ashley/Leo	NIGEL HASTINGS
Gale	SOPHIE ROBERTS

Subsequent UK tour cast 2015:

Tom	RUSSELL DIXON
Blanche/Mrs Miller	SARAH STANLEY
Roz	KRYSTLE HILTON
Lindy Kuze/Mrs Kuyper	BROOKE KINSELLA
Russ	RICHARD STACEY
Lance/Sean	LEIGH SYMONDS
Ashley/Leo	NIGEL HASTINGS
Gale	ELIZABETH BOAG

Director: ALAN AYCKBOURN
Design: MICHAEL HOLT
Lighting: JASON TAYLOR
Fight Director: ALISON DE BURGH

CHARACTERS

BLANCHE HOLGATE – 40s
TOM HOLGATE – her father, a retired judge, 70s
RUSS TIMMS – a clergyman, 30s
GALE DEVONNE – an entrepreneur, 30s
ASHLEY KUYPER – a neighbour, 40s
ROZ PERKINS – a schoolgirl, 16
LINDY KUZE – an escort, mid 30s
LANCE – an enforcer, 40s
MRS MILLER – a choreographer, 40s
LEO AXMINSTER MP – 40s
SEAN MCKINTYRE – a journalist, 30s
MRS KUYPER – a constituent, 70s

SETTINGS

A neutral area. Onstage at the start there are eight randomly placed pieces of furniture to be used throughout the evening, rearranged accordingly with additional coverings and minimal trimmings added or subtracted as are considered necessary. These are: –

A desk, a swivel chair, a sofa, a low coffee table, an armchair, a small table (dining height) and two upright chairs.

There is one interval after the third play (whichever that is) and minimal breaks between the others.

***

Suggested doubling for a company of eight: –
BLANCHE / MRS MILLER
AND
LINDY / MRS KUYPER

THE AGENT

CHARACTERS

GALE DEVONNE – an entrepreneur, 30s
LANCE – an enforcer, 40s
ASHLEY KUYPER – a neighbour, 40s

Scene: One morning in a room in Gale's apartment which serves as her office.

The spare room in GALE's *town centre apartment which she has made over as her business office. Morning.*

A sofa with coffee table, an armchair, a desk with a phone, a swivel chair and two upright chairs. A table near the window.

One door.

GALE *enters.*

She is speaking into her mobile as she enters.

GALE *(into her phone)* ...No, listen darling...this is your very first professional audition, darling, and this man is a very, very important producer, indeed...believe me, in British film circles you can't get bigger than Leo Axminster...yes, even him...now it's important, darling, you swallow your pride and do exactly what he asks you to do...within reason... you're not to glare at him or swear at him or for God's sake head-butt him, as you've been known to do in the past... Best behaviour now. Your career rests in the balance...if he likes you...that's a big door opened for you...yes!

The front door buzzer sounds. GALE *rises, still talking, and moves slowly to the window.*

Good... Good... Oh and, darling, don't forget to ask him for my casting fee, will you? ...No, no, that's not the way it works, not at all. When you get to my level, darling, they pay me for the privilege... Yes.

As she looks out of the window, the buzzer sounds again.
GALE, *seeing who it is, reacts alarmed.*

Oh my God! Darling! I must dash, now. All the phones here
are ringing like crazy. It'll be Hollywood waking up. And,
darling, remember you're Rose now. <u>Rose</u> Perkins. Not Roz.
No, well you'll get used to it. Forget Roz. Dreadful name.
No ring to it. Just think of it on the marquees! 'Bye now!

She ends the call and immediately speed dials another.
She moves to the window again and looks out anxiously.

(into phone) Come on, Lindy... Answer! Answer it! You can't
be asleep at this hour, you lazy cow! ...Come on! *(Getting a*
response) Oh, thank God! Lindy, it's Gale...yes... I've been
trying you for ages... Yes, lucky you... Listen... Lindy, are
you awake now? ...You sure? Because this is urgent...

Her flat's doorbell rings this time. GALE *now looks*
anxiously towards the door.

I need somewhere for a night or two... No, I've still got this
flat – It's just I've got the decorators in at the moment, darling,
there's tins and ladders everywhere... It's a nightmare...yes –

A heavy knocking on the front door.

Yes, you can hear them now...yes... Listen, Lindy, would
you mind awfully if I came round right now? ...No, I really
don't mind at all, darling, I'll take you as I find you...we're
mates, aren't we...?

More heavy knocking.

Just hark at them, will you! What are they up to in there?
Listen, I can be there in about –

More knocking. GALE *moves to the door as she speaks.*
She is now contemplating possible escape routes. Her
options are apparently limited.

Lindy! Need to go! I have to go!

She hurries out of the door, still clutching the phone.

Offstage, a sudden final loud thud, and a crash as the front door is splintered off its hinges and falls to the hall floor. A cry as GALE *re-enters, staggering backwards, as if she has been given a hefty shove.*

She loses her footing and sits in the middle of the floor.

(winded and slightly shocked) Oh, God!

The doorway is filled by LANCE, *a big man in his forties. Seeing him,* GALE *covers her head protectively with her arms, presenting a defensive bundle.*

Don't hit me! Please don't hit me! Please!

LANCE *(cheerfully)* Good morning, Gale. Hope we didn't wake you. Come on. Up you get then.

GALE I can't. I think my legs are broken.

LANCE Come on. That was only a gentle push. *(Stepping forward and offering his hand)* Here, allow me.

GALE *(misinterpreting the gesture, protecting her face)* No!

LANCE Come on, Gale, I'm not going to hurt you... Up you get!

She cautiously accepts his offer of help. He takes her hand and pulls her to her feet.

(smiling) I won't hurt you. Not yet, anyway...

GALE's *other hand is still clutching her phone. He takes it from her, whilst retaining his grip on her other hand. From her expression, he is clearly holding it very tightly.*

(as he takes the phone) Allow me. *(Into the phone)* Hallo...who am I speaking to? ...Oh, Lindy! 'Morning, Lindy. Unusual for you to be up and about at this time. This is Lance. I'm afraid Gale's unable to come to her phone at present... No, she's fine, Lindy. She's in good hands. We're here to take care of her. Now, Lindy, you go back to bed now, like a good girl,

get your beauty sleep, alright? Remember, you're working tonight, aren't you, darling?

He ends the call and tosses the phone on to the sofa, smoothly taking GALE's *other hand as he does so.*

Didn't realise you two were friendly, you and Lindy. She didn't tell us that. Naughty girl. Could have saved us a lot of trouble finding you. Have a word with her later. She must be a rare friend for you, Gale. In your hour of need...

GALE *(tensely)* Would you let go of me, please...?

LANCE ...and I can assure you, Gale, this is certainly your hour of need, girl.

GALE You're hurting my hands!

LANCE Mr Simmons is very cross with you. You're in his bad books, you are. Naughty girl, aren't you? Going to get a smacking, I wouldn't doubt.

He gives her hands an extra squeeze for good measure.
GALE *whimpers, half in pain, half in fear.*

GALE I'll find the money, I promise. I know exactly where I can get it. Two more days, I swear...

LANCE Too late, Gale. Too late. Really. Time is up, girl. Mr Simmons trusted you. He gave you his trust. You've hurt him deeply, Gale. You've wounded him. I'm afraid it's payback time, sweetheart. If someone hurts him, chances are he'll hurt them. And guess who that's going to be, Gale? Guess who? *(Squeezing her hands)* Can you guess?

GALE *(with a squawk)* Me!

LANCE *(squeezing again, his face close to hers)* Yes, you, Gale! You!

GALE You're breaking my hands, you bastard!

LANCE *(pulling her towards the door)* Come on! Off we go!

GALE *(resisting)* Will you let go!

LANCE *(continuing to pull)* Come on! Want me to carry you, then, do you?

GALE If you don't let go, I'll scream the place down. I swear I will! There's other flats in this building. They're all occupied, you know.

LANCE This block's full of pensioners, we checked.

GALE They've all got phones though, haven't they? They hear me screaming, they'll have the emergency services round here before we reach the front door.

LANCE Why should they bother? They probably won't even hear you.

GALE You haven't heard me scream. Now please, Lance, let go, please. I won't be any trouble. I'll come with you, quiet as a mouse. I promise. But please, just let go. *(Slight pause)* I give you my word. *(In a tiny voice)* Please.

LANCE *looks at her, decides to trust her and releases her hands.* GALE *gasps and winces as the pressure is released. She rubs her hands to restore the circulation.*

(flexing her hands tentatively) I'm going to be covered in bruises, now.

LANCE Would you just look at this place! Get a load of all these pictures, then! Who are all these people, anyway?

GALE They're clients.

LANCE Clients?

GALE I'm an agent, a theatrical agent, aren't I?

LANCE And these are all your clients?

GALE *(guardedly)* Most of them. Some of them are.

LANCE *(studying one of them)* Including this one? Who's this then? Looks like Chuck Norris.

GALE It is Chuck Norris.

LANCE He's not a client of yours, is he?

GALE No, of course not.

LANCE Chuck Norris. Great personal hero of mine, he is.

GALE That figures.

LANCE Got all his films, I have. Pirated versions. Come on then. Downstairs. Car's waiting.

GALE No wait, I need the toilet. I need the toilet first.

LANCE You can go when you get there.

GALE Unless you want me to mess up your nice car. Mr Simmons' lovely car.

LANCE *(grudgingly)* Alright. I'm coming with you, though.

GALE No, you're bloody not. Listen, there's no way out of this place. Apart from the front door. What's left of the front door, anyway. I'm not going anywhere, am I?

LANCE Be quick, then.

GALE Look, if I'm not coming back here, which presumably I'm not, then I need to put a few things together first. It won't take ten minutes.

LANCE You've not got ten minutes –

GALE Listen, there's only the front door of the building, isn't there? The fire escape's at the side there. You can see it from the road there, where you're parked. Well, then? Where am I going to go? Please, Lance, five minutes. I promise I'll be good. Promise.

LANCE *(moving to the door)* Five minutes, then.

GALE *(meekly)* Thank you.

LANCE What have you got to pack that's so important?

GALE *(a trifle embarrassed)* Oh, you know, just – women's things. Personal.

LANCE Five minutes, no more. Go and have your pee.

LANCE *goes out.*

GALE *(as soon as he's gone, savagely)* Bastard!

She moves to the desk, intending to use the phone. LANCE
returns.

LANCE Hey –!

GALE *(jumping, guiltily)* What?

LANCE I'll be out there in the car. My colleague, Denzil, will
be in the road downstairs just outside the main front door
at the bottom of the fire escape.

GALE Yes, alright.

LANCE *moves to the desk, and pulls the land line cable
out of the wall.*

LANCE Sorry about that.

GALE *glances at her mobile, still on the sofa.* LANCE
intercepts her look and picks this up on his way out.

I'll look after this too, shall I? Not that I don't trust you.
Get going.

GALE *waits till she's sure he's left the flat. She checks
the door. She dithers undecided.*

GALE Oh, God! Please, God! Don't let me die, please. I promise,
I'll be ever so good in future. Don't leave me here to die.

*She goes to the door again and contemplates her escape
options. She looks at the window. She opens it. The
sound of distant traffic. She looks down. And steps back,
hastily. It is evidently a very big drop.*

(closing her eyes) Oh, no!

*She comes to a decision. She goes to the desk and, opening
a top drawer, finds a black hair tie with which she
scrapes back her hair, in preparation for action. She*

*peeks out of the window again. She drags the table closer
to the window. She climbs on it. She takes several deep
breaths, as though steeling herself to step out onto the
outside ledge.*

(softly to herself) Come on, Gale. One small step! Come on,
then! You can do it, girl, you can do it. Go, Gale!

ASHLEY, *a man in his forties, cautiously sticks his head
round the door.*

(unaware of him) Go, Gale, go! One...two...three! Step! *(She
fails to do so)* No. Here goes! One...one, two...three! No!
This time! One. Two-three! Step! Come on, you silly bitch!
This time for real! One-two-three. Here I go!

ASHLEY I really wouldn't advise that, you know.

At the sound of his voice, GALE *panics and nearly loses
her balance.*

GALE *(startled)* What? *(wobbling on the window ledge)* Keep
away! Keep away, do you hear? I will, I promise I'll jump!
I'm not joking. If either one of you lays a finger on me – I'll
jump, I swear it! I'll –

She sees ASHLEY *properly for the first time.*

Who are you? Who the hell are you?

ASHLEY Ashley Kuyper, from downstairs. Number 3C. I have
to advise if you jump from there, it's a considerably long
way down.

GALE What?

ASHLEY We're on the fourth floor here, you know.

GALE Who are you? What are you doing here?

ASHLEY I'm from downstairs. Number 3C. Directly below
you. All this clattering and banging. Mother is directly
underneath, you know. She was having a little lie in this
morning. After her mishap. You've put paid to that.

GALE I'm sorry.

ASHLEY What's going on up here, anyway? What's the matter with your front door? It's lying on the hall floor, completely off its hinges.

GALE Yes, I know.

ASHLEY They're not going to like that, the managing agents, they're not going to smile on that, you know. They don't even like you re-painting them. Unless it's an approved colour. Now, come down from there this minute. Come on, down off the table. Get a grip on yourself. I tell you one thing, if you jump from that window, if you don't clear the building, properly, there's a likelihood you'll land on mother's window box. And she certainly won't love you for that. Now, come along, down you come! *(Extending a hand to assist her)* Here.

GALE *hesitates.*

Come on then. I'm not going to bite.

GALE *(nervously)* You won't squeeze my hand, will you?

ASHLEY *(laughing)* Not unless you'd like me to. I will if you like. Only joking, of course.

GALE, *assisted by him, climbs down.*

GALE Thank you.

ASHLEY That's better. Now sit down. You sit here. Compose yourself. Get yourself orientated.

GALE *sits on the sofa. He sits beside her.*

Now, listen to me. I don't know what it was you were trying to do, what was the cause of it, but it was extremely foolish. You're an attractive young woman, full of life and expectations and the last thing you want to do is to throw that all away in one rash, foolhardy gesture...

GALE What are you talking about?

ASHLEY Believe me, I've found, in this life, it can get bad. It can occasionally get you down a bit. But it can never get so bad that you need to jump out of a window and kill yourself. There's always another option.

GALE I wasn't trying to jump.

ASHLEY Weren't you?

GALE I was trying to escape. To find a way out.

ASHLEY Same thing, different wording. Think of your nearest and dearest. Think of them. You need to think of them.

GALE Who?

ASHLEY The ones you'd be leaving behind. Your loved ones. Think of them.

GALE I haven't got any loved ones. Why do you think I'm in this mess, in the first place? If I had any loved ones, they'd be here. Loving me. Helping. I'm all on my own here.

ASHLEY Oh, dear. How sad! Now come on, you're not on your own. I'm here now. Look on the bright side. I may not be much but at least I'm somebody. There is also my mother downstairs as a last resort. She is incapacitated at present or she'd be up here in person. She had an accident crossing the road. She tripped in a pothole. It's disgraceful, you know, the state of these roads. We intend to complain...

GALE Listen, sorry to interrupt but can I use your mobile?

ASHLEY My what?

GALE Your mobile! You do have a mobile phone, don't you?

ASHLEY Oh, no. Mother and I don't bother with those. Think of the bills.

GALE You don't have a mobile? The one man in the bloody country who doesn't have a mobile...

ASHLEY Mother has a panic button round her neck. But that's just for emergencies.

GALE This is an emergency. We're running out of time. They'll be back in a minute. They're coming back –

ASHLEY Who are coming back?

GALE The men waiting out there! The people who are going to kill me.

A pause.

ASHLEY *(concerned)* Oh, dear. You are in a bad way, aren't you?

GALE They're just out there. Believe me. Please. Look out of that window. Go on, look. Please. Go on, look!

ASHLEY *(warily)* This window?

GALE Yes of course that window! There's only one bloody window.

ASHLEY Alright! Alright! You stay there, don't move, now.

GALE Where would I go?

ASHLEY *moves cautiously to the window, as if he's expecting a trap.*

ASHLEY You've got a lot of photos here, haven't you?

GALE I'm an actors' agent. They're mostly pictures of my clients.

ASHLEY Very impressive. *(Noticing a photo on the wall)* This is Chuck Norris, isn't it? You don't represent him, do you?

GALE *(impatiently)* Only in the West End. Please, would you look out there and tell me what you see.

ASHLEY What am I supposed to be looking for?

GALE There's a car. Parked on the other side of the street. A big black one. You see it?

ASHLEY Oh, yes. Very smart. A Mercedes E220, if I'm not mistaken. Last year's plates.

GALE Can you see the driver?

ASHLEY No. It's got those tinted windows. I can't see any driver.

GALE No?

ASHLEY There's a man standing leaning against it, though. Big bloke. He seems to be cleaning his nails with something. Possibly a knife.

GALE There you are then. Now do you believe me?

ASHLEY Hardly breaking the law, is he? Doing his manicure in the street. Not very hygienic but still...

GALE There's another man, just outside the front door. Watching the fire escape. Do you see him?

ASHLEY Oh, yes. *(Craning)* I can just about see him. Top of his bald head, anyway. Quite a big head.

GALE You should see the rest of him. Now, are you going to help me...?

ASHLEY Alright. You have my attention. So far, so good. Two big men outside. Apparently waiting for someone. This is a bit like one of those television programmes, isn't it? The ones Mother likes. Well, we both enjoy them, really. They always get their man, don't they? At the end. Except when it's in two parts. When they carry on the story for another episode. Then it's 'Previously on CSI...'

GALE Please, you have to help me! Please!

ASHLEY Sorry. Get me going on those, I'm away. Mother's even worse than I am. Both of us chattering away for hours on end. I'm sorry. Go on, then. Tell me the rest of it. I'm all ears.

GALE What do you mean, the rest of it? I haven't time for that. We don't have any time!

ASHLEY Now, don't get excited. We have all the time in the world. Those two out there, they're not going anywhere, are they?

GALE *(shouting impatiently)* Of course they're not going anywhere! That's the whole point, you stupid fucking idiot!

ASHLEY *(sternly)* Now, now, now, now! Shouting at me won't get you anywhere, will it? If you don't control yourself, unless you behave, young lady, curb that tongue of yours, I'm going straight back downstairs again. Then where will you be, eh? So no more of that, alright?

GALE *(meekly)* I'm sorry.

ASHLEY Mother's due for her drops in a moment, anyway. No, there's no point in shouting at people like that, is there? Using language? Gets you nowhere in life. No wonder you don't have any friends. A little politeness, a little consideration for others. Good manners cost nothing now, do they?

GALE *(despairingly)* Oh, God, help me! Someone help me, please!

ASHLEY I'm trying to help you. That's precisely what I'm trying to do. Now there's two men out there, waiting. Waiting for you, you say? Am I correct so far?

GALE Correct.

ASHLEY And why are they waiting for you?

GALE *(wearily)* I've told you, because they want to kill...

ASHLEY *(with her)* ...because they want to kill you. Yes, we've established that. But there's a flaw in this story line, you see? They're the ones who battered down your front door, right?

GALE Yes...

ASHLEY And then, presumably they confronted you? Threatened you?

GALE Yes...

ASHLEY And then they went off downstairs again? To wait?

GALE Yes...

ASHLEY Now, tell me this. If they wanted to kill you, why didn't they kill you here? Instead of going downstairs again?

GALE Because Mr Simmons wants to see me first. Mr Simmons wants to see me... Oh, God, it's too complicated to explain...

ASHLEY Ah! Mr Simmons! Now we have a Mr Simmons! Who's Mr Simmons?

GALE He's – Mr Simmons is – There's no time to explain now!

ASHLEY Is that the man down there, is that Mr Simmons?

GALE No! He's not Mr Simmons. They work for Mr Simmons...

ASHLEY Then who's Mr Simmons, then?

GALE He's Mr Simm – Oh, what does it matter?

ASHLEY I have to say, I'm not altogether convinced by this story. There's a considerable number of loose ends.

GALE *(fiercely)* Are you going to help me, yes or no?

ASHLEY *(stubbornly)* Not yet! I'm saying, I have yet to be convinced.

GALE Yes or no? Otherwise leave me alone and piss off!

ASHLEY *(sternly)* Now, this is your final warning. You have been warned. Mother would have washed your mouth out with soap long ago, young lady. Now, behave!

GALE Sorry.

ASHLEY If I'm going to help you, I need you to tell me the whole truth, the complete story from beginning to end. Without a barrage of bad language. Alright?

GALE What's the time? We're running out of time.

ASHLEY You never hear them swearing on CSI, now, do you? And, believe me, they often have very good reason to swear, some of the scrapes they get in to. Far greater than yours.

GALE *(weakly)* Oh, God! Are they still out there?

ASHLEY *(checking the window)* Yes, still out there. He's eating something now. *(Reacting)* Oh, no, no! Don't just throw it down like that. Look at that! Just threw the wrapper on the pavement! *(Returning to her)* Right. Deep breath and away you go. From the very beginning, now. Whole story.

GALE *(fairly rapidly)* My father is an accountant, a successful freelance accountant, a few years ago he was approached by a group of businessmen, a consortium, headed by Mr Simmons who offered him a considerable sum of money to handle their books in return for strict confidentiality... *(She pauses for breath)*

ASHLEY Their books. Yes, yes, I'm with you so far. Carry on!

GALE *(continuing at the same speed)* ...that is until a few months ago when my father discovered that the whole thing was a cover and that these men were part of an international drugs cartel, involved in extortion, wide scale prostitution and murder at which news my father was horrified...

ASHLEY He would be...

GALE ...because till then he'd never suspected and he tried to distance himself from the whole thing immediately...

ASHLEY ...naturally, he would do...

GALE ...but it turned out he already knew too much and so they threatened him...

ASHLEY ...in order to protect their interests. They would, of course...

GALE ...he's been on the run from them ever since and they're still trying to find him and now they're planning to use me, his daughter, as a lever to get to him and he set me up in this flat and made me change my name to Gale Devonne...

ASHLEY What's your real name then?

GALE ...Deirdre Wilkins...

ASHLEY ...that's a nicer name, Deirdre...

GALE ...only now they've managed to track me down and they're planning to use me to get to my father and because we both know too much about them, in the end they're going to kill us both and that's it, in a nutshell! *(She finally pauses for breath)*

ASHLEY Good heavens! What a tale!

GALE Now, will you help me, please?

ASHLEY I most certainly will, Deirdre! May I call you Deirdre?

GALE No! Call me Gale. That's my cover name.

ASHLEY Right. Gale, Gale, Gale. I'll try and remember. I'll do my best to help anyway! I prefer Deirdre. You look much more like a Deirdre than a Gale. I'm Ashley, by the way. That's my real name.

GALE Yes, you look like an Ashley. What are we going to do, then?

ASHLEY Yes. We need a plan, don't we? I don't fancy tackling those two down there. Not head on. I don't think I'd stand much of a chance against those two...

GALE Probably less than I would.

ASHLEY No, we need guile. We must resort to guile, Gale. That's our only option. My word this is exciting, isn't it? I can't wait to tell Mother...

GALE At the rate you're going, you'll be lucky to see her again.

ASHLEY They've covered the fire escape, you say?

GALE Yes, the other one, Denzil, he's got that covered.

ASHLEY *(to the window)* So, how about this way? Is this the way you were trying just now?

He climbs cautiously on to the table.

This is secure, I take it? Only I'm not so good with heights. I have to get Mother to change the light bulbs – now then... *(Looking down)* Oh, my word, I see what you mean.

GALE There's a narrow ledge along there, do you see?

ASHLEY Oh, yes. It's very narrow, isn't it? I seem to recall they tried doing this – in one of the earlier CSI episodes. I think it was the New York series – with Mac and Stella. With near disastrous consequences...

GALE I haven't a clue what you're talking about! Look, you see? I thought once we stepped out on to that ledge, we might just be able to work our way along just as far as the next window there, do you see? If we managed to climb through that, we'd be laughing.

ASHLEY Yes. I see what you mean. It's quite a distance, though. To that next window. What's through that next window by the way, do we know?

GALE It's – Oh God, it's my kitchen, isn't it? It's my kitchen! We'd still be in this flat.

ASHLEY Ah! A flaw in the plan!

GALE I can't even think straight. What's the matter with me? What about the other way? What's it look like if we went the other way?

ASHLEY There is no other way. That's the end of the building. No, I'm afraid that all looks very impractical. Much too narrow. Sorry. We could climb up.

GALE Up?

ASHLEY Up to the roof, perhaps?

GALE The roof? What's the point of that?

ASHLEY That's what they tend to do. When they're trapped. I remember in CSI Miami, David Caruso – you don't happen to represent him by any chance, do you? No, too much to hope for – him and the one with the very high voice, Emily whatsername –

GALE Would you shut up about fucking CSI!

ASHLEY Now, now, now...

GALE *(hysterically)* Just get me out of here! Please, get me out of here! Please!

ASHLEY I'm trying to think. Stop shouting and swearing. That's not helping at all. Not one little bit!

GALE I'm sorry. I know you're trying to help. We've never met before and you're doing your very best. And you've got a mother downstairs who needs looking after and you've gone out of your way to help me and I've every reason to be grateful to you. But I have to say you are the most irritating person I have ever met in my life!

A silence. **ASHLEY** *is rather hurt.*

I shouldn't have said that. I'm sorry. But please understand, in a few hours time I'm almost certainly going to die and I hope it will be quick and not too painful but you must understand at this moment in time, I'm in a bit of a state. And the only person I have left in my life to rely on is you... *(She starts to cry)*

ASHLEY *(quietly, with new resolution)* You're not going to die. I'll see to that.

GALE *(sniffing)* I'm not?

ASHLEY As my late father would have put it. Nil desperandum, Ashley. We're going to find a way out of this. We're going to get you out of here, if it's the very last – Don't you worry, Deirdre!

GALE Gale.

ASHLEY Gale. We'll do it, never fear. Trust me. *(Taking her hand firmly)* I'm here.

GALE *(wincing)* Ow!

ASHLEY Oh, sorry. Did I hurt you?

GALE Just a little.

ASHLEY Don't know my own strength, do I?

He smiles at her. She smiles faintly in return.

GALE Listen – I said horrible things to you and I shouldn't have said them. And I didn't mean them, truly I didn't. I was just overwrought and I – Sorry.

ASHLEY No, that's quite alright. I've no illusions. Why do you think I still live with Mother? She's the only person in this world who's prepared to put up with me. And she says I drive her mad occasionally.

GALE Was there never anyone – else in your life?

ASHLEY Oh, yes. At one time. All forgotten now. He went his own way. It was quite amicable.

Slight pause.

Well, Gale, I've been wracking my brains, casting my mind back, trying to recall how they dealt with this situation in previous episodes. Two helpless, unarmed people, trapped on the fourth floor of a building, no way out, with two very large violent men down below who are probably armed. And invariably, on TV at least, this type of situation tends to end in violence. Usually with an intense gun battle. But since neither of us, so far as I know, has even so much as a pen knife...

A pause.

GALE No. Well, thanks for trying, anyway. You did your best.

ASHLEY Usually, you know at this point in the narrative, just before all hell breaks loose, the man and the woman – it's usually a man and a woman, isn't it?

GALE *(smiling)* Yes. The butch hero and the token tottie...

ASHLEY *(laughing)* Hardly that in our case. Quite the reverse in many ways...but usually, while they're waiting, they tend to gaze deeply into each other's eyes and then – I used to find this very irritating when I was little – I used to shout at the screen, "Oh, do please get on with it!" – but the hero and the woman usually stand there, on the very verge of

Armageddon and one or other of them would lean forward and then – as if on impulse – they'd...

GALE *leans forward and kisses him on the lips.*

GALE Like that, you mean?

ASHLEY Very much like that. Thank you very much.

GALE My pleasure.

They stare at each other.

(smiling) Roll on Armageddon, then! *(Looking out of the window)* Oh, God, no, he's crossing the road! They're on their way up! What are we going to do? What are we going to do?

ASHLEY *(casting around for ideas, inspired)* Er... Your hair!

GALE What?

ASHLEY That thing in your hair! The thing holding your hair! What's it called?

GALE You mean the tie?

ASHLEY Give it to me!

GALE Why? What are you doing?

ASHLEY Quickly! Give it here!

GALE *removes the black hair tie pinning back her hair.*

GALE *(muttering as she does so)* This is hardly the moment to do my bloody hair, surely?

ASHLEY Here! Give it to me!

She does so.

Now, hands behind your back!

GALE Behind my back?

ASHLEY Come on, do as you're told!

GALE *(complying)* What are you doing?

LANCE *(offstage, calling)* Gale! Gale!

GALE *(sotto)* Oh, God!

ASHLEY Together! Put your wrists together! Quickly!

> GALE *obediently holds her wrists together behind her.*
> ASHLEY *slips the hair tie over them.*

GALE What on earth are you doing?

ASHLEY Now, twist your hands!

GALE What?

LANCE *(offstage, nearer)* Gale, your time is up. Come on now.

ASHLEY Twist them! Twist your hands!

GALE *(twisting her wrists)* Would you tell me what's going on?

> LANCE *enters.*

> *As he does so,* ASHLEY *gives* GALE *a shove forward. Her*
> *hands temporarily pinned behind her back, she collides*
> *with the desk and folds double over it, face downward.*

ASHLEY *(with new found authority)* Alright! That's enough
from you, madam!

LANCE *(simultaneously, as he enters)* Gale!

GALE *(winded by the desk)* Uh!

ASHLEY *(to LANCE)* Alright, friend, stand down! I'm taking
over from here!

LANCE *(startled)* Who the hell are you?

ASHLEY Serious crime squad, DCI Clapton! J Division.

LANCE You leave her! She's ours!

ASHLEY Yours? Who are you, then, sunshine?

LANCE Never mind. She's coming with us.

ASHLEY Listen, sonny, I've got an armed SWAT team outside
in plain vehicles, ready and waiting. Raring at the bloody

bit! I've got a dozen sharp shooters on the rooftop out there. Desperate to take a shot! You want to argue, you argue with them, mate. This little bitch is mine.

GALE *(lifts her head indignantly)* Wha –?

ASHLEY *(shoving her down again)* Oh, no you don't, madam! Don't you try that! This one's ours, mate! We've been hunting her down for weeks.

LANCE What's she done, then?

ASHLEY What hasn't she done, more's the point. One of the great con women, this one! Wanted in six countries! Join the queue, feller! Come on you, Gale, Deirdre, whatever you call yourself! Take a tip from me, sunbeam. Make yourself scarce. Don't get caught up in this lot. Or my governor will nail you to the wall as an accessory. Take a friendly tip from me and piss off out of here! Go on! Off you go! Go! Go! Go!

LANCE *retreats.*

LANCE Right! Right no problem!

ASHLEY I can handle this little two-timing tart!

GALE *pops her head up again.* ASHLEY *immediately shoves her down again several times. Her head bangs on the desk.*

GALE Ow! Ow! Ow! Ow!

LANCE Bloody hell!

LANCE *goes out hurriedly.*

ASHLEY *stops. They wait.*

GALE *(breathless)* Jesus!

ASHLEY *(himself again)* Sorry about that! Pardon the language. You alright?

GALE You're worse than him. You men!

ASHLEY Sorry. I had to trawl back a bit further. Then I recalled an old episode of The Sweeney where they did something similar. One of Mother's favourites. She's got all the DVD's. She's a great fan of John Thaw.

GALE *(still dizzy)* Great. Can't wait to meet her. Has he gone?

ASHLEY *(at the window)* Yes. He's crossing the road with the bald bloke. They're getting back in their car. Can't wait to get out of the place. Can you manage there?

GALE *(untwisting her temporary handcuffs)* Well, I have to say, that was inspired. You were brilliant. I've got a splitting headache but at least I'm still alive. Brilliant.

ASHLEY Would you care to come downstairs for a moment? Have a cup of tea with Mother? I know she'd love to meet you, say hallo.

GALE Yes, sure. Why not?

ASHLEY Besides, if I told her what's just happened she'd never believe me. She'd accuse me of making it all up. She's terrible like that. Never believes a word you say.

GALE Runs in the family, then? *(Starting to re-do her hair)* You didn't believe a word I told you either, did you? My father, the accountant, on the run from the drug barons. His innocent daughter held hostage...

ASHLEY Ah, yes, one of my favourite episodes, that was. I must have seen it dozens of times with repeats. I always enjoy it. You coming?

GALE *(finishing her hair)* Coming. You lead on.

ASHLEY Come on, come and meet Mother, Deirdre. *(As he goes)* Are you fond of biscuits by any chance, Deirdre... It's safe to call you that now, isn't it? – Only we've got this brand new tin of mixed creams from Auntie Shirley... Wonderful selection...

He goes out.

GALE *lingers for a second.*

GALE *(incredulously, to herself)* Bloody hell, Deirdre! What have you got yourself into now, girl?

As she goes.

The lights fade to: –.

Blackout.

THE JUDGE

CHARACTERS

TOM HOLGATE – a retired judge, 70s
LINDY KUZE – an escort, 30s
LANCE – an enforcer, 40s

Scene: Evening. The sitting room of a hotel suite.

A desk with a swivel chair. On the desk, a framed, fifty-year-old photograph of an attractive young woman in her twenties.

Across the other side of the room, a sofa with cushions and a coffee table plus an easy chair. Centrally, a table with a white cloth, laid up for dinner for two and two dining chairs.

One door into the room leading to an upstairs landing. Another door leads to the bedroom and bathroom.

LANCE, a big man in his forties, is currently standing by the table. He is dressed as a hotel waiter. He studies the table. He adjusts the cutlery. He appears slightly apprehensive, giving anxious glances towards both doors.

In the background, the TV set drones on. Another local news interview with **LEO AXMINSTER MP.**

LEO *(his* VOICE*)* ...now you're talking to a born countryman here, Jon. Anyone who knows me will tell you I'm country stock, born and bred. My grandfather was a farmer, as was my great-grandfather and so was my great-great-grandfather – my family are all from solid farming stock and I assure you I yield to no one in my love of the British countryside –

VOICE In which case, Mr Axminster, surely –

LEO *(his* VOICE*)* – my family have grown up over generations tilling the soil, experiencing first hand the joy, the tears, the excitements and the disappointments, that only a true farming community can know about –

VOICE In which case, Mr Axminster, surely you'll concede that –

LEO *(his* VOICE, *laughing)* No, no, Jon, please be fair! Allow me to finish – Marianne has made her point, very forcefully and colourfully and I've no doubt sincerely – and I fully appreciate her concerns. No one in their right mind who purchased their home in the middle of a green field site, wants to look out over acre after acre of concrete and red brick – but I can assure her that isn't going to be the case. Not a bit of it. That, if I may say so and with due respect to Marianne, is simply alarmist talk! Now if she'd only taken the time to read –

VOICE But the report states categorically –

LEO *(his* VOICE*)* – if she'd only taken the time to read –

VOICE – the report states very clearly and unambiguously –

LEO *(his* VOICE*)* – to read the report in its entirety, there are provisos which I promise go a long way to addressing her concerns – I can put her mind at rest on that. This talk of the mass destruction of hedgerows, the loss of indigenous wildlife, the uprooting of trees is simply not true. Nothing could be further from the truth. I repeat, not one single healthy tree is at risk. If you study the facts you'll find that, quite to the contrary, we are actually planting more trees. In the past five years, I'm proud to say, as a result of our New Green Britain initiative, we will have planted more trees than the previous government managed in twenty years of disastrous office. I mean, personally I adore trees, I grew up with trees all around me and I learnt from a very early age to respect them. My own garden is filled with trees. Many of which I got down on my hands and knees and helped plant myself...

During this: –.

LANCE *(calling to the bedroom)* Lindy! Come on, get a move on then!

LINDY *(offstage)* Alright! I'm coming! These bloody hooks...

LANCE *(calling)* He'll be here in a minute!

LINDY *(offstage)* Alright! Alright! Alright! Who designed this fucking thing, anyway?

LANCE shakes his head.

After a moment, the phone on the desk rings.

LANCE hurries to answer it.

LANCE *(into phone)* Yes? ...Where are you, Denzil? In the foyer? ...Well bring him up, then... We're all ready here... *(With a glare towards the bedroom)* As ready as we ever will be... Yes, bring him up... Oh...and Denzil! Use the service lift. Not the main one... Yes, the one round the side, opposite the bar... See you in a minute.

He hangs up.

(he marches to the bedroom doorway, calling) Come on! He's here now!

LINDY *(offstage)* Oh, shit!

LANCE *(calling)* He's on his way up. Come on, get your arse out here, girl!

He grabs the remote from the coffee table and kills the unseen TV sound.

(as he does so, to the TV) And you can shut up and all!

As he does this, LINDY *enters from the bedroom. Although she is in her 30's, she is dressed rather formally in an authentic period evening gown dating back some fifty years or more. Her hair and make-up are done in a suitably matching style. Although the overall impression is of someone rather beautiful,* LINDY *walks stiffly and awkwardly. She is clearly unused to what she is wearing.*

LINDY *(presenting herself)* Well?

She stands. LANCE *studies her.*

LANCE Turn round.

LINDY *revolves on the spot.*

LANCE *picks up the photograph from the desk and holds it up, comparing it to* LINDY. *There is a striking resemblance between the two.*

That's not bad. Not bad at all.

LINDY I can hardly breathe.

LANCE What, the dress too tight?

LINDY Everything's too tight.

LANCE It's your size. They made it in your size.

LINDY It's not just the dress... It's all this – other stuff.

LANCE Other stuff? What other stuff?

LINDY This stuff underneath. What have I got to wear all that for? It's like I'm in a bloody suit of armour under here.

LANCE It's authentic. Molly said you had to wear it. She says it's authentic.

LINDY It's orthopaedic. Besides, he's not going to know, is he?

LANCE He might. He might want you to take your kit off later.

LINDY I thought this was just dinner?

LANCE Yes, well, after dinner...you never know. Be prepared.

LINDY I'm only being paid for dinner with him. That's what was agreed. Anything after that is extra. I'm charging extra. If we go in that bedroom, we're in overtime.

LANCE You'll be paid! You'll be paid.

LINDY Yes, well...

LANCE Mr Simmons will see you right. Don't worry. Listen, he's paying you a lot of money for this job, Lindy. You'd better make sure you earn it, girl.

LINDY I'll earn it. *(Half to herself)* Every bloody penny of it, if I know Simmons.

LANCE You are clean, I take it? I take it you're clean?

LINDY Yes, I've just had a bath.

LANCE Don't be funny. Whilst you were wallowing in there, you haven't been indulging in any dodgy substances, have you?

LINDY No.

LANCE You sure?

LINDY Positive. I had a sniff of body lotion, does that count?

LANCE I have to say I have severe doubts about you for this job, Lindy.

LINDY Yes. So have I.

LANCE We should have had Gale for this job, she'd have been ideal.

LINDY Yes, well Gale's unavailable. She's done a runner, hasn't she?

LANCE We'll catch up with her, don't worry. Then she's in real trouble. This is an important job, Lindy. Get this one right, you'll be on your way. Mr Simmons doesn't forget. He remembers the ones who do right by him. He's a generous man. He likes to show his gratitude. You fuck this one up and you're dead meat, girl.

LINDY That's encouraging. Nothing like a bit of motivation, is there?

LANCE Now, you remember who you're meeting? You remember his name?

LINDY Tom. His name's Tom.

LANCE You remember your name?

LINDY   Nina.

LANCE   No, not Nina. Nonie. Nonie! Bloody hell, Lindy, how many more times, girl? You've got a sodding head like a sieve, haven't you?

LINDY   Nonie!

LANCE   And who's Nonie?

LINDY   His wife.

LANCE   His <u>late</u> wife. You're meant to be his late wife.

LINDY   Don't know why he wants to meet his late wife. Most men I know can't wait to get shot of them.

LANCE   I'll be watching you like a hawk, Lindy. Constantly.

LINDY   Where you going to be then? Crouching behind the sofa?

LANCE   No, I'm the waiter.

LINDY   The waiter? That's why you're all dressed up, is it?

LANCE   I'm your floor waiter for the evening.

LINDY   You're not a waiter, though.

LANCE   That's how Mr Simmons wants it. Anyone can be a waiter.

LINDY   Can't wait to see that. Sloshing soup all over the place. I should have worn my raincoat.

LANCE   You're not having soup.

LINDY   What are we having, then?

LANCE   To start with you're having Lobster Biscuits.

LINDY   Lobster biscuits?

LANCE   That's what the menu says.

LINDY   What the hell are lobster biscuits?

LANCE   Posh food. Wait and see, you ill-bred birdbrain.

LINDY   Then what we got soup spoons for?

LANCE To eat your fucking lobster biscuits with, you ignorant cow!

The doorbell chimes.

Alright! That's it! He's here. Here we go!

He moves to the door. LINDY *takes up her position across the room.*

Ready?

LINDY Ready.

LANCE And for God's sake, Lindy, talk proper.

LINDY *(talking proper)* Absolutely, darling. *(She flashes an artificial smile)*

LANCE, *at the doorway, adjusts the lighting level via a dimmer switch so the room gets slightly darker.*

He then admits TOM, *a retired judge in his seventies. He moves with difficulty with the aid of a stick.*

LANCE Come in, Sir Thomas, do come in. *(To someone outside)* Thank you, Denzil, I'll take over from here. Mind your step, sir, it's a little bit uneven there. Can you manage alright, Sir Thomas?

TOM I can manage, I can manage. *(Looking around)* Is this it?

LANCE Courtesy of Mr Simmons. The best room in the house.

TOM The John of Gaunt Suite.

LANCE Sorry?

TOM That's what it says on the door there. The John of Gaunt Suite.

LANCE Ah, well. Full of history, this place. Steeped in history.

TOM *(staring at the ceiling)* Reckon he might have stayed here, do you? John of Gaunt?

LANCE Oh, very possibly. I understand they've had all type of celebrities staying here over the years. Andy Williams, Alan Titchmarsh...

TOM He died of syphilis, you know.

LANCE Alan Titchmarsh?

TOM John of Gaunt. Aged fifty-eight.

LANCE Oh, tragic. Well it comes to all of us, Sir Thomas, in the end, doesn't it?

TOM Syphilis? I bloody well hope not. *(Looking around)* Well, this'll have to do, I suppose... *(Seeing LINDY for the first time)* Oh, dear God! Nonie?

LINDY *(softly)* Hallo, Tom.

TOM Now that's very good. You're very good. She's very good, isn't she?

LINDY *(modestly)* Thank you.

TOM You look – almost an exact likeness...the spitting...you could almost be her. So far as I can remember her. Back then, in those days. Come closer, darling, step into the light.

LINDY *steps forward.*

That's better. Beautiful, my dear. Stunning.

LINDY Thank you.

TOM You're an absolute cracker, do you know that? As we used to say. You don't mind being called a cracker, do you?

LINDY Call me what you like. You're paying.

TOM Only I know girls these days, they prefer not to be called things like that. I don't know why. *(Smiling)* There's no harm in being called a cracker, surely?

LINDY *(laughing)* I've been called a lot worse.

TOM *(laughing)* No, I don't believe that for a minute.

LANCE Would you care for me to open the champagne, Sir Thomas?

TOM Champagne?

LANCE With Mr Simmons' compliments.

TOM Yes, of course. Crack it open. Fancy a drop of champagne, do you, darling? I remember you used to love it.

LINDY I still do.

TOM You used to drink it like water, you little devil.

LANCE *(busy with bottle)* She still does...

TOM Shall we sit down then, shall we? Care to sit down, would you?

LINDY Thank you.

They both sit on the sofa. LINDY *with difficulty.*

LANCE *busies himself opening the bottle.*

TOM Champagne, eh? Well, Danny's certainly pushing the boat out tonight, isn't he? Knowing his pushes, the boat won't even clear the jetty, but it's the gesture that counts. Champagne in the John of Gaunt Suite at the Station Hotel. That's as big as it gets with Danny.

LINDY Who's Danny?

TOM Sorry, Danny Simmons. Don't you know him?

LINDY Oh, yes. Mr Simmons.

TOM Devious bastard, Danny. Can't trust him an inch. I've known him for ages and ages. I used to be a High Court judge you know, in the old days.

LINDY *(slightly uneasily)* Oh, really?

TOM Retired now. Long ago. But before that I was a QC. A criminal QC. I had the near impossible task of successfully defending Danny Simmons on more than one occasion. So the bugger owes me. He certainly owes me.

LINDY What was it he did, then?

LANCE *(swiftly intercepting)* Champagne, Sir Thomas!

TOM Oh, thank you – whatsyourname – *(To* LINDY*)* What's his name again?

LINDY Lance.

TOM Lance.

> LANCE *has poured one of the glasses with very little.*

LANCE *(offering this to* LINDY*)* Madam?

LINDY *(staring at her glass)* Thank you.

LANCE *(offering the full glass)* Sir Thomas?

TOM Thank you.

LINDY Excuse me. Waiter.

LANCE Madam?

LINDY I'd appreciate a full glass, if you don't mind.

> LINDY *and* LANCE *exchange looks.*

> *She hold out her glass defiantly.*

TOM What? Is that all you've poured her? God, the girl wants a decent glassful, man. Pour her a proper one, you scoundrel.

LANCE Sir Thomas. *(He takes back her glass)*

LINDY *(smiling)* Thank you so much, waiter.

LANCE *(smiling)* Madam.

TOM *(to* LINDY*)* You can tell he works for Simmons, can't you? *(Calling)* Hey, you! Lancelot!

LANCE Sir?

TOM How long have you been a waiter?

LANCE – er...

LINDY Five minutes.

TOM Yes, so it would appear. Well, take a tip from me, never pour half measures for the ladies. They don't appreciate it. The least they'll do is complain and if they've had a few they'll probably dot you one. And serve you right. My wife here certainly would. Now apologise, at once.

LANCE returns with a full glass.

LANCE *(through gritted teeth)* I do apologise, madam.

LINDY Thank you, waiter.

TOM Now piss off, there's a good chap, and leave us alone. From now on, we'll pour our own.

LANCE *(going reluctantly)* Yes, sir. *(Stopping in the doorway)* Regarding dinner, Sir Thomas, do you want me to serve it –?

TOM *(barking)* Don't bother us with dinner, man! We'll call you when we want our dinner! We'll have dinner in our own good time! Now bugger off!

LANCE looks daggers and goes off.

One needs to be firm with these people, you know.

LINDY Oh yes, one certainly does.

TOM *(raising his glass)* Here's to you, my darling.

LINDY Cheers, darling!

They drink.

Mmm! Nice.

TOM Not bad. Could be a shade cooler.

LINDY Possibly. A shade cooler.

TOM Non-vintage, too, isn't it?

LINDY Yes, delicious.

TOM No, you never could tell, could you? Downed the stuff like water, you monkey, didn't you? Could never tell the difference, could you?

LINDY *(smiling)* No...

TOM *(smiling)* You're so – like her – it's eerie. And yet you're not like her at all. It's very odd, sitting here with someone I used to know so well – so intimately – and yet at the same time I'm with a person I can't remember at all. It's odd.

LINDY *(dropping back momentarily into her old self, gently)* Just tell me what you want me to do, love?

TOM I'm losing you, you see, Nonie. You don't mind me calling you Nonie, do you, darling? I know that's not your real name. I know that. I've no idea what your real name is, I don't even want to know it...I'm sorry.

LINDY It's alright. You call me Nonie...

TOM You're gradually slipping away from me, Nonie. This bloody memory of mine. It's causing me to lose you, you see. There's more and more each day, I can no longer remember of you. Less and less of *us*. I can feel it gradually slipping away. Do you follow?

LINDY Yes, I think so...

TOM I have fewer and fewer of those precious pictures left now. The tide's slowly coming in, darling, covering up a little bit more every day. Each time I wake up, I find my strip of beach is getting narrower. I can't remember my childhood at all now. Not a single minute of it. My schooldays have totally disappeared. Well, they're not important. Can't be. I went back to the place recently. Terrible barn. I can't possibly have been happy there. No, the earliest memories I have, as of now, are the early days after our wedding. I'm alright from there on. I can remember the accident, your accident, very clearly. How could I forget that? But I woke up a couple of days ago and I couldn't remember our first meeting. Not a single detail. Isn't that terrible? Not to recall our first meeting! The day I first clapped eyes on you, my darling, caught my first glimpse of your face, of your sweet loving face. That's too much to bear, it really is.

He sits sadly. A silence. LINDY *is visibly moved by this.*

LINDY *(tearfully)* Oh, dear... *(She rises)*

TOM You alright?

LINDY Yes, I just need a drop more of this...

TOM *(struggling to get to his feet)* It's alright, darling. Don't you...

LINDY *(refilling her glass)* No, I can do it. You want some more?

TOM *(sitting back down)* No, I don't know whether I should. These days, you know...

LINDY *(returning with the bottle)* Come on. Keep me company.

She refills his glass.

TOM Oh, well. Thank you. I'll probably fall asleep.

LINDY *moves away, replaces the bottle in the ice bucket and sits on an upright chair some distance from him.*

What are you doing sitting over there?

LINDY It's more comfortable here. This – dress – is a little bit tight. That sofa's rather low. *(She takes one or two deep breaths)* I'm fine here. I must say, if I'm really as much like your wife as you say I am...

TOM Uncannily like her. Like Nonie. Sometimes.

LINDY ...she must have spent a lot of her time being short of breath.

TOM *(puzzled)* No, I don't remember that about her. I do recall though, when she was young, she had a slightly higher voice than you.

LINDY *(going up an octave)* Really? Like that? That better?

TOM No, don't bother, please. That's horrible.

LINDY *(normal again)* So, what are we doing? Recreating your – our early days together, are we? Is that the plan?

TOM In so far as we can.

LINDY Going to be a bit tricky, isn't it? I haven't a clue what happened and you can't remember a thing about it.

TOM We need to be inventive, darling. Creative, you see. Artistic.

LINDY Artistic? I don't know if I can do that. I've never been into that.

TOM No?

LINDY I used to have a friend who was artistic. She did this number with a snake. She was artistic.

TOM *(mystified)* A snake?

LINDY Till they took it off her. She's retired now. But I'm not into artistic. Sorry.

TOM No, come on, don't lose heart! We can do this. Between us. Let's concentrate. Forget all about snakes. We must have met – I must have met you...where did I first meet you, then? Any ideas?

LINDY In a pub.

TOM No, no! Not a bloody pub! A party! It must have been at a party. Thrown by a mutual friend.

LINDY What mutual friend?

TOM What's it matter? I can't remember any of them, anyway. No, someone who said, 'Tell you what, let's invite our old friend Tom along. He's at a loose end. Bit lonely, studying day and night for his law exams. And, yes! We could also invite Antonia, couldn't we –? Good idea!'

LINDY Who?

TOM Antonia. That's you. Always known as Nonie. So far as I know. Or maybe that was just my name for her? Nonie. *(A slight panic)* Oh, God, I can't remember now! I can't remember anything, you see! Ridiculous idea of mine! This is absurd!

LINDY Come on, then! We're at this party. I'm sitting here. I'm rather shy. I'm all on my own...

TOM Shy?

LINDY ...I don't really know anyone here...

TOM You can't possibly have been shy. Nonie was never shy. She was always the centre of attention.

LINDY I'm sitting here surrounded by people, then. All these big, tall men...

TOM ...I was always the shy one, if either of us was –

LINDY ...I'm sitting here with all these handsome, tall men surrounding me, crowding me for attention – and suddenly I catch a glimpse of this shy, awkward boy staring at me with this intense look on his face. He seems out of place here. Standing with a glass in one hand and a bundle of dusty law books under his arm –

TOM No, no, no. I'd never have taken those to a party, I wasn't that shy, for God's sake...

LINDY (slightly impatiently) Well, I don't know. Something else under your arm, then. A bowl of crisps? A table lamp? The hostess? A set of bagpipes? ...I don't know, do I?

TOM Alright! Alright! Just a glass in my hand. Nothing at all under my arm. And I catch your eye...

LINDY ...and I catch yours...

TOM And slowly, I work my way across the room towards you...

LINDY And all the other men, sensing something important is going on...

TOM ...they all melt away...

LINDY ...and we're suddenly all alone...

TOM ...no one else in the room...

LINDY ...just us.

Slight pause.

TOM *(shyly)* Hallo.

LINDY *(shyly)* Hallo.

TOM I'm Tom.

LINDY Antonia. Everyone calls me Nonie. Hi.

TOM Hi.

LINDY What are you up to at present, then?

TOM I'm a law student. Apprenticed to this firm in the city. Newbold, Cook, Bentley and Wennick.

LINDY Oh how fascinating! That must be such fun!

TOM It is. Terrific. Mostly. And you, what about you? How are you planning to fritter your life away?

LINDY Oh, I haven't a clue, really. I've only just come down from Oxford.

TOM Oh, really? What were you reading?

LINDY *(vaguely)* Oh, you know, books. Physics books...and things. You know. Masses of them.

TOM Wow! Brainy, then.

LINDY *(modestly)* Sort of.

TOM Which college?

LINDY What?

TOM Which college were you at?

LINDY *(totally stumped)* Oh – the old one, you know. That one. You know.

TOM Oh, really? Do you mean New College?

LINDY No, I said. It's the old one. I just said.

TOM New College is an old one.

LINDY Is it?

TOM Founded in 1389.

LINDY Oh.

She gets up and moves away.

(despairingly tearful) No, I can't do this any more. Sorry. You need my friend Gale. She could do it. I can't do it. I don't know anything about these things. I don't even know what I'm talking about half the time. Dressed up in these suffocating clothes, talking in a stupid voice, pretending to be someone I never am, not in a million years.

I'm sorry I can't help you, Tom. I'd like to but I can't. I'm sorry, you need a bloody psychiatrist, not a fucking call girl! *(Quieter)* Sorry, mate.

A silence.

LANCE *appears in the doorway.*

As he enters, LINDY *moves swiftly and refills her champagne glass.*

LANCE *(slightly suspiciously)* Everything alright?

TOM Yes, thank you. Perfectly fine.

LANCE Would it be alright for me to serve you your dinner? Only –

TOM Yes. You can serve dinner. We're ready now.

LANCE *(with a look at* LINDY*)* You sure you're –?

TOM Dinner, please, Lancelot. Immediately!

LANCE Yes, Sir Thomas.

LANCE *goes out.*

TOM *(gently)* It's alright, my darling. Don't worry. Don't worry now. We're doing well. We're both of us doing very well.

I'm sorry, I panicked you. I should never have asked you those sort of questions. Stupid of me. How could you be expected to know?

LINDY No, well. I don't know the answer to anything, me. Nothing at all.

TOM You know what's important. The things that matter.

Pause.

I'll tell you something interesting, shall I? Just now, when you started shouting and stamping about the place...you were closer then to Nonie, more like her, than you've been all evening.

LINDY Did she used to yell a lot, then?

TOM She was inclined to. From time to time. I think I drove her nuts occasionally. Just now, I almost believed she was in the room with me.

LINDY *(smiling faintly)* Got something right then, didn't I?

LANCE *enters, pushing a trolley upon which are two soup bowls and a covered tureen, bread rolls etc.*

TOM Ah-ha! Dinner is served. Do you want to sit that side, Nonie darling?

LINDY *(sitting at the table)* Lovely.

TOM I must say, I'm about ready for this, aren't you?

LINDY Rather!

TOM Now, Lancelot, what have we got here?

LANCE *(with a sour look at LINDY)* Soup, Sir Thomas.

LINDY *(flashing LANCE a smile)* Oh, super. I adore soup.

LANCE *serves the soup into the bowls with a ladle. He does a fair to middling job of it.*

They watch him. He prepares to serve them.

TOM Well, he managed to get most of it in the bloody bowls, anyway.

LANCE *makes to serve* TOM *first.*

Serve my wife first, please.

LANCE *(doing so)* Madam?

LINDY Thank you, Lancelot.

LANCE *(serving* TOM*)* Sir Thomas.

TOM *(examining his bowl)* Now, what have we here? *(He sniffs)* I suspect a bowl of delicious lobster bisque. Am I right?

LANCE Yes, sir. Lobster bisque.

LINDY *laughs.*

LANCE *gives her his death ray look.*

TOM What's that? What is it, my darling? What's so funny?

LINDY *(barely able to control herself)* Nothing.

TOM Are you not a fan of bisque?

LINDY *(wiping her eyes)* I was rather hoping for some biscuits.

TOM Biscuits?

LINDY Yes.

TOM You want biscuits, my darling? You prefer biscuits? Then you shall have biscuits, my precious. Waiter, take all this away! Bring us some biscuits.

LANCE Biscuits? You want biscuits?

TOM Biscuits, man, biscuits! You've heard of biscuits, haven't you?

LANCE You want biscuits with it?

TOM No. Instead of. We want biscuits instead of this. Take all this away. Bring my wife a large tin of biscuits. Come on, chop-chop! A giant family tin! Can't you see the woman's starving?

LANCE *(alarmed, hastily clearing the soup)* Yes, Sir Thomas.

He starts to wheel the trolley off again.

TOM *(calling after him)* And with those biscuits, kindly rustle up two mugs of cocoa.

LANCE *(bewildered)* Cocoa? Yes, Sir Thomas.

LINDY Chop-chop!

LANCE *goes off with the trolley.*

TOM You like cocoa, darling, I seem to recall.

LINDY Yes. Whatever.

TOM Well, that's the end of dinner, I think. No point in having cocoa and biscuits sitting here at the table, is there? Shall we sit somewhere else?

LINDY Sure.

They rise. She sits by the desk.

TOM *(indicating the sofa)* Perhaps back on the – oh, no – I'll sit here and you – *(Seeing she is already seated)* – you can sit over there.

She refills her champagne glass again.

TOM *sits on the sofa.*

LINDY I haven't been much use, have I?

TOM Well. The way I looked at it, it was always going to be a bit of a long shot, wasn't it? Truth is, I was expecting rather a lot. Too much. What's gone, after all, is gone.

LINDY *(anxiously)* You're not going to ask for your money back, are you? Only I need the money, you see.

TOM No, no, no. You've done your bit. More than your bit. Thankfully, I can still remember most of Nonie. Our later years, anyway. Perhaps that's all I was intended to have left of her. Not the early years at all. Her youth.

LANCE *re-enters with a half empty tin of assorted biscuits on a tray.*

LANCE Biscuits, Sir Thomas.

TOM *(waving at the coffee table)* Thank you. Put them down there, will you?

LANCE *(as he does so)* I got them off the night porter. His private supply. Cocoa may be a minute or two. We took the kitchen a bit by surprise.

TOM Quick as you can, then.

LANCE *goes out.*

Biscuit, darling?

LINDY No, thank you, darling.

TOM No?

LINDY Don't feel like one just now.

TOM You're the one who wanted the bloody things, not me. Typical. I'm going to have one, anyway.

He opens the tin.

Ah-ha! One or two goodies left in here. Eluded the hungry digits of the night porter. *(Selecting one and tasting it)* Mmm! Very good. Sure you won't, darling? No? What are you dreaming about over there, then?

LINDY You know, I remember now. I remember the first meeting, that's all.

TOM The first –? Oh, I see. Our first meeting?

LINDY It wasn't at a party at all. It could never have been at a party. Not that sort of party, anyway. I was right in the first place. We did, we met in this pub!

TOM A pub? Did we?

LINDY I was very young, about sixteen. I was in this pub in King's Cross. All on my own –

TOM On your own? Aged sixteen?

LINDY Right.

TOM In a pub in King's Cross? What on earth were you doing there?

LINDY I was working.

TOM Working?

LINDY As a – as a barmaid.

TOM Sixteen. Under age. Totally illegal.

LINDY Didn't seem to bother anyone. And you came up to me and started chatting me up and we got friendly, you know – and I – as I say, I was really young then – I wouldn't do it now – but I let you talk me into giving you – you know – a free drink.

TOM Good heavens! That could have got you into all sorts of trouble.

LINDY It did. My – my manager, manager of the pub, he wasn't at all pleased with me, giving it away for nothing. And he was going to belt me. And you stepped in. And then you and him, you both went round the back to have it out. And you sorted him good and proper, you did –

TOM I did?

LINDY Christ, you should have seen him. And then you said to me, what about it, then? Fancy a trip to the seaside, do you? And I said, what the hell, I've lost my job now, anyway. So you wired up a car and away we went.

TOM This doesn't sound like me at all. Fighting in pubs! Wiring up cars? Thank God I wasn't caught. Finished my legal career before it started.

LINDY Nah, we weren't caught! No way! Too quick for them! You were driving that fast. I was clinging on, scared shitless.

It was amazing! Never gone that quick. Screaming round those streets. Middle of the night.

TOM Heavens! Where did we finish up? At the seaside, you say? Brighton, was it?

LINDY No. Not Brighton. Southend.

TOM Southend?

LINDY Yes.

TOM I don't remember ever going to Southend.

LINDY We used to go there with my mum when we were little and then, when I was older, when I was sixteen I went there, this time with – with you.

TOM Why on earth would I take you to Southend?

LINDY You didn't. I told you I wanted to go there.

TOM I don't recall any of this... Are you sure we –?

LINDY No, wait! Haven't finished. And when we got there. After we'd ditched the motor, we had breakfast. Burger and fries. And then we walked on the beach, put our toes in the water. And then you wanted a go on the slot machines, you know. I didn't. But you wanted to. I thought they were dead boring. But you insisted – and then you ended up working one of those with a little crane that tries to pick things up, you know –

TOM Oh, yes. I know the ones you mean...

LINDY – only half the time it doesn't pick them up at all. It just drops them again. It's the way they're made. But you were really set on picking up this ring for me – this pretend diamond ring – plastic, probably – and you spent a fortune, just trying to get it – we could have bought a real one with what you spent on that machine –

TOM God! Fancy wasting my money on that!

LINDY No, most of it was my money, you bugger. You didn't have none of your own, you.

TOM Oh lord, strapped for cash as usual, was I?

LINDY You could say that.

TOM Well, after all, I was a student. My allowance probably hadn't come through – Anyway, carry on. I was playing this wretched machine and then what happened?

LINDY Then finally you did it!

TOM I did?

LINDY You picked up the ring and it dropped down and it slid out the slot at the bottom. And we both went, yeah!

TOM Yeah!

LINDY Yeah! And we went off to celebrate. Had fish and chips in this café. Pot of tea. Bread and butter. And we were sitting at this table in the window and you – I had to laugh – you suddenly went down on one knee and you asked me to marry you. And I said, oh, yes please. You know, joking.

And everyone was looking at us in this shop. And out in the street, staring at us through the window, you know. All of them laughing, some even started clapping. But we didn't care because we were laughing too. *(Reflecting fondly)* That was a good moment, that was.

TOM *(incredulously)* I proposed to you in a fish and chip shop in Southend?

LINDY You did.

TOM With a ring made of plastic?

LINDY I've still got it somewhere. Saved it.

TOM What happened then? After I proposed in Southend?

LINDY We both went off to this pub on the seafront and got completely rat–arsed on Special Brew. And afterwards we went down the beach again, in the dark by the pier to have it off, only you threw up before we could do it. So we both fell asleep on the beach. And when I woke up in the morning, you'd legged it.

TOM *(incredulously)* Legged it?

LINDY You'd gone. Scarpered.

TOM *(deflated)* Oh, dear. How terribly sad. And that was the end of it? It can't have been, surely?

LINDY I was very young. I was stupid in those days. Wouldn't do that now.

Slight pause.

TOM No, no, hang on! I remember now! I remember! You haven't finished, have you? You haven't finished the story, girl! No, if you recall, just after you woke up on that beach, I hove into view with a couple of beakers of hot tea – which I'd bought with my own money – from this pie stall. You remember that bit, surely?

LINDY *(vaguely, a little bemused)* Oh, yes...really?

TOM And then I said to you, how about a good hot bath, Nonie old girl, and a proper sleep? So we both checked in at this charming little hotel on the seafront and the woman gave us her best room, overlooking the sea... You remember that bit, surely?

LINDY Probably. What happened then?

TOM Well, what usually happens, you know. Great big double bed, you and me. Then we kept on seeing each other, more and more frequently. And finally, you took me home to meet your parents –

LINDY Oh, no... No! My parents? I'd never have done that.

TOM No? Well, I certainly took you home to meet my parents, anyway.

LINDY What did they make of me, then?

TOM They were completely captivated, my darling. You charmed them out of the trees!

LINDY That's nice. Glad they liked me. I was afraid they wouldn't.

TOM And in due course we got married.

LINDY In white?

TOM Oh, yes, the full works.

LINDY Bridesmaids? Maids of honour? Pages? Lots of confetti?

TOM Buckets of the stuff.

LINDY Lovely. Happy ending, then?

TOM Very happy. Very, very happy, my darling.

They both reflect for a moment.

She sits beside him on the sofa.

LINDY That alright then? Filled in the gap, has it? That do it for you, then?

TOM Oh, yes. That does it for me. Thank you. Point is, does it do it for you?

LINDY Oh, yes. It does it for me, too.

LANCE *enters with a tray with two mugs.*

LANCE Cocoa, Sir Thomas.

TOM Splendid! About time. Cocoa, Nonie old girl?

LINDY *(smiling)* Lovely, darling. Can't think of anything nicer.

As LANCE *serves them their cocoa they continue to sit smiling at each other as the lights fade to: –.*

Blackout.

THE NOVELIST

CHARACTERS

BLANCHE HOLGATE – 40s
TOM HOLGATE – her father, a retired judge, 70s
RUSS TIMMS – a clergyman, 30s

Scene: A rainy night in the leaking conservatory attached to the Holgates' house.

*A conservatory attached to the **HOLGATES'** house. A sofa with coffee table, an armchair, a desk, a desk chair, a table, two upright chairs. Two doors, to the house and the garden.*

Rain is heard on the roof. Various receptacles are dotted about the room to catch the drips from the leaking roof, including a three-quarter filled bucket. We hear the drips occasionally throughout the current rainstorm and, from time to time, after the deluge has stopped.

TOM, a retired judge in his seventies, is waiting anxiously for his guest. Glancing at his watch and giving the occasional impatient look towards the conservatory outer door. He goes and listens at the door to the main house. He moves with difficulty with the aid of a stick.

A tapping on the outer door. TOM hobbles over to unlock it. Before he reaches it, there is further knocking.

TOM Just a minute!

He unlocks the door. RUSS, a clergyman aged in his thirties, falls into the room. He is somewhat rain-sodden.

Heavens above! Come on in... What a night!

RUSS *(breathlessly)* Thanks, Tom! Sorry, I'm a trifle late. Not a good night for driving. Your lane was blocked. I had to come the long way round...

TOM Blocked?

RUSS Tree blown down, I think.

TOM No. Not another one...

RUSS I had to loop round and come through Tussock. *(Indicating his coat)* Mind if I take this off?

TOM Oh, do. Anywhere you like...

RUSS *(removing his coat)* I parked in the drive. By the front door. I hope that's alright?

TOM Fine.

RUSS Only you specified I should come round the side. Through the conservatory, here. Not to use the front door. I must say, it all sounded a bit mysterious.

TOM Yes.

RUSS 'See me first, whatever else you do...' What's it all about? *(Finally removing his coat)* There, that's better! What can I do to help? I'm intrigued.

TOM Well, it's nothing too... Yes, well, no. It's everything, really. I don't quite know where to...

He tails off. A silence. **RUSS** *waits, still holding his coat.*

...begin. No.

RUSS No. What shall I do with this?

TOM It's just that I'd prefer it if you didn't run into Blanche, that's all – Talk to her. Not till after you'd spoken to me – oh, just sling it down over there somewhere – No, frankly, Russ, the point is, I wanted a word with you first, you see... I wanted a... I wanted a...word. Yes.

RUSS Yes?

TOM *(glancing up)* Would you just look at that. The state of that roof. I ask you...

RUSS *(looking up, concerned)* Yes. You've got – you've got one or two leaks up there, haven't you?

TOM One or two... Certainly coming in... Look, you can see where it's coming in there, you see?

RUSS Oh, yes, it's certainly coming in. Look at it. Perhaps you ought to get it fixed? Before it gets any worse. In my experience those sort of things can only get worse. The longer you leave them, the worse they tend to get. Yes, look, this bucket's filling up...nearly full. Yes.

TOM Yes. Mind you, it's been like that since the day they put it up, this conservatory...

RUSS How long ago's that?

TOM *(vaguely)* Oh. Thirty five years. At least.

RUSS Ah, well. Probably not still under guarantee then?

TOM I really can't remember. Long term memory's fading a bit I'm afraid. *(Tapping his head)* Like a book, you know. Book of your life. It's as if someone's tearing out all my early pages, one by one. Every time I wake up, I find there's another bit missing. Someone sneaks by in the night, takes away another one. It used to be engraved in stone – *(Tapping his head)* – here, you see? In solid granite. Only now it's as if it's been sand-blasted away.

RUSS How awful for you.

TOM Mostly, you know, when people get older, a lot of them, so they tell me, they tend to lose the short term memory – forgetting where they put their damn glasses, what they did yesterday, or even what day it is today – But what they tend to get in return, you see, the older they get, is their early childhood images. Memory's parting gift before you pop your clogs, like a forgotten photo album up there in the attic of your head. All as clear as if they were taken yesterday. Something for you to treasure, dwell on in your old age. A consolation for every other bloody awful thing you have to put up with in old age. But the point is, I've no longer got an album, it's been mislaid.

RUSS Well. You never know – maybe – you'll come across it.

TOM Maybe. Will you hark at that rain.

They listen. RUSS *waits.*

RUSS *(at length, tentatively)* – er... Tom...

TOM No, the point is Nonie – Antonia – we always knew her
as Nonie, you know – Nonie was the one who wanted this
conservatory. It was her idea. We must have a conservatory,
darling. Everyone round here's got a conservatory except for
us. We need one to sit in. I said to her, listen, my darling,
we've got forty-four other perfectly good rooms we can sit
in, what's the point of having another one?

RUSS Ah...

TOM She got her way, of course. As she always did. She got
her bloody conservatory. Hardly had a chance to sit in it,
though, before she...

Slight pause.

RUSS Oh, yes. Tragic.

TOM Nowadays, nobody sits in it. In summer it gets unbearably
hot and in winter it's either freezing cold or soaking wet.
Like now. *(Gazing around gloomily)* Just look at it. Coming
in everywhere.

A silence.

RUSS I – er...

TOM What's that?

RUSS Was there a special reason you wanted me to call round,
Tom? I take it you weren't seeking my advice about leaking
roofs... *(Laughing)* Because I'm afraid I'm not an expert...
(He laughs)

TOM *is silent.*

A pause.

(seriously) I take it it's about Blanche? Since you didn't
want me to talk to her. Before I'd seen you? I take it this
has something to do with your daughter?

TOM Yes. It does.

A silence. **RUSS** *waits.*

RUSS How is Blanche, by the way? Still on with her writing? I haven't seen her for ages. Not since the funeral. My, that was – heavens – that was a couple of months ago now, wasn't it? I've been meaning to – I meant to look in on you both. Time races by, doesn't it? ...I did mean to drop in. See how you were coping with your loss, both of you. She seemed to take it very... Haven't seen her for ages, Blanche.

TOM No, I can't say I have.

RUSS *(laughing)* You haven't? I find that hard to believe, Tom. It's not as if you aren't both living in the same house. You must run into each other occasionally. Even in a place this size.

TOM She tends to avoid me. Chooses to go her own way. Suits me. I go mine.

RUSS I see.

TOM Since the funeral, you see, we've hardly spoken.

RUSS I sensed she and her mother were especially close...

TOM Yes, they were very close. Always were. Ever since Nonie's accident. Blanche nursed her every day after that. Practically every day. Twenty-eight years ago now. Since Nonie's fall.

RUSS Poor Blanche. That must have been exhausting for her. Mind you, doesn't she have her job? Her part time job? Working for our local MP? That must provide a little variety, I'd have thought.

TOM I can't say I'm too happy about that. Never have been. Her working for that chap. Leo Axminster MP.

RUSS Because of his politics, you mean? Yes, he's quite right wing, isn't he?

TOM Right wing? He makes Genghis Khan look like a Lib Dem. No, it's not his politics so much as his personal life. Very suspect.

RUSS Oh, have you heard something? That is worrying.

TOM Mind you, you expect that, don't you? He's an MP, isn't he? Most of them are bent as hairpins. He's sexually rather dodgy. Into fillies, apparently.

RUSS Fillies?

TOM Girls. Young ones.

RUSS Oh, sorry. My mind was on – horses, for some reason –

TOM Horses? He's not into horses as well, is he? My God, that's even more worrying if he's into livestock.

RUSS No, no, I – er...didn't mean. No, no.

Another silence.

TOM They claimed she'd been drinking, of course. That she was drunk.

RUSS That Blanche was drunk?

TOM No, not Blanche. Blanche has never been drunk in her life. Her mother. That Nonie was drunk.

RUSS Oh, dear, how awful...

TOM Everyone assumed that was the reason for her fall. Nonie's fall was due to drink. She was drunk.

RUSS Well, it's a sad fact of life, isn't it, that at the first opportunity, people are always ready to jump to conclusions, aren't they?

TOM No, they were absolutely right. She was. Completely off her face. In those days, that was Nonie's natural state most of the time. Thirty years ago, that was more or less her norm. In those days, she wasn't a happy woman. Still, she never touched a drop since then. There's nothing like falling down the main staircase there and breaking your neck for sobering you up, is there? *(Wearily)* I don't know, Russ. Maybe I was to blame for her unhappiness in those days. I don't know.

RUSS Blanche's unhappiness?

TOM No. Nonie's unhappiness. Do listen, old chap.

RUSS Sorry. Is that why you wanted to see me, Tom?

TOM What?

RUSS To talk about some sense of guilt?

TOM Guilt?

RUSS To discuss a sense of guilt? You feel that in some way you were the cause of Antonia's – Nonie's – accident? That you were in some way to blame?

TOM Blame for what?

RUSS For her accident.

TOM Her accident? That had nothing to do with me. I wasn't even here at the time. No, the reason she fell was she was an alcoholic. Had been since the day I married her. Or so I rapidly discovered. She came from an entire family of alcoholics. You can't blame me for that. Nothing to do with me. No, I was referring to the woman's unhappiness. Whether I might possibly...had I been more...been slightly more... I don't know, I could just have perhaps made her happier.

RUSS Ah, well. We can all of us look back, can't we, in retrospect...?

TOM But then again, it was two way. She didn't make me very happy, either. She could have given me a better time, too, if she hadn't been completely plastered most of the time. No, six of one, Russ. Fair do's. But then that's marriage for you, isn't it? Hell on both sides.

RUSS (doubtfully) Yes.

TOM Certainly our marriage was. Towards the end. (Looking up) Oh, dear God, look, it's coming in there as well! I've only just noticed it. See?

RUSS Tom, you don't feel that – that unhappiness – her unhappiness might have been connected in some small way – I'm not saying directly – but in some tangential, oblique sort of way to her drinking?

TOM No.

RUSS No?

TOM I can't see the connection. Her drinking was a completely separate issue. I've told you, it was hereditary. Nothing to do with me. In her genes. Nonie got hopelessly drunk on our wedding day. Long before I had a chance to make her unhappy. Ended up flat on her back in a flower bed.

RUSS *(laughing)* Oh, dear. Not a promising start, then.

TOM I'm sorry. I don't want to talk about all that. Past history.

RUSS You don't?

Silence. A rumble of thunder.

TOM *(looking up at the roof)* I think this is set in for the night, you know.

He continues to stare at the ceiling.

RUSS *(at length, gently)* What was it you did want to talk to me about then, Tom? If it wasn't Antonia – Nonie? On the phone you sounded very agitated. You said you needed to talk to me on a personal matter of some urgency. What was that, Tom?

A pause. **RUSS** *waits patiently.*

TOM It was... I needed to... I thought... I couldn't think of anyone I could...and then I thought of you, Russ. Not just because you're a clergyman, you understand...but as a...you know...someone I could... I could turn to... I thought you might...well...be the very person... I needed.

RUSS *(somewhat touched)* Thank you, Tom.

TOM *(staring at him)* But now I'm not so sure you are.

RUSS Ah. *(A pause)* Well, in that case, I'd better be... If...

TOM *(suddenly, getting increasingly agitated)* Listen, I might as well tell you, anyway. Where's the harm? There's probably not a thing you can do about it but I need to tell someone. Dear God, I have to tell somebody! You're probably worse than useless but it's you or nobody! It's –

A bell, inside the desk, rings loudly.

Both men jump.

(staring at it in horror) Oh, my God! Oh, my God, she's hidden it in here now! She's put the bloody thing in here!

RUSS What is it?

TOM That bell! She's brought it in here now!

RUSS What bell? Is it the front door?

TOM No, it's <u>her</u> bell. It's Nonie's bell. Her remote bell. She had it by her bed. That damn woman keeps moving it around!

RUSS *(confused)* Who does? Nonie's moving it around?

TOM No, not Nonie! Blanche! My daughter keeps moving it round the place. Ringing it when I'm least expecting it. Hides it in my bedroom. Ringing it in the middle of the night. She even hid it in the bloody toilet. I nearly...

RUSS Well, surely you can switch it off? Disconnect it?

TOM You think I haven't thought of that?

The bell rings again, continuously this time.

(agitated) She's at it again! Switch it off! Switch the thing off!

RUSS *(alarmed, searching)* Wait a minute, it's here in the desk somewhere.

He opens several desk drawers and rifles through them in search of the bell which continues to ring.

TOM *(covering his ears)* Somebody, turn the confounded thing off!

RUSS *(over the din)* Wait! Wait! Wait! *(Locating the bell at last)* Ah!

> RUSS *holds up the bell, a remote radio unit, which is still ringing, louder now.*

What shall I do with it?

TOM Get rid of it! Just get rid of it! Stop it! Stop the thing!

> RUSS, *indecisive, stands holding the bell like an unexploded bomb. It continues to ring. Finally, he plunges it into the bucket of water on the floor. It stops. A silence.*

Thank God for that!

RUSS I think I've probably ruined it.

TOM Oh, don't worry, she has others. She buys them in bulk off the internet. I've seen whole trucks from Amazon full of them, reversing up the drive.

RUSS Oh, dear! That is worrying.

TOM I've removed the batteries, I've thrown them into the fire, I've jumped up and down on the bloody things, I've even hurled them into the road out there. And still they come. The woman's relentless.

RUSS Blanche? You're positive Blanche is doing this?

TOM Who else? There's no one else in the house it could be, is there?

RUSS I can't believe she'd be doing it deliberately. Why on earth would she do that? To her own father? No, there's a more rational explanation, there must be, Tom. It's a wireless bell, you say? It's interference perhaps? From somewhere?

TOM *(sardonic)* From the spirit world, you mean? My late wife trying to contact me from beyond the grave, perhaps? By ringing her bell? That's what Blanche would have me believe, anyway.

RUSS I was thinking of something more mundane. Like a rogue TV remote control unit –

TOM No, Russ, let's face it, the reason I wanted to see you is Blanche has gone totally potty. Off her head. Ever since the funeral.

RUSS Oh dear, really? Since the funeral, you say? Yes, Blanche was...a trifle... Yes. Mind you, it was a lovely ceremony. You spoke very movingly, Tom. Most people found it deeply touching.

TOM Apart from my daughter. Did you hear her? You must have heard her, halfway through?

RUSS I think most of us put that down to an extreme expression of her grief.

TOM What? Screaming with laughter? Completely put me off.

RUSS No, no...

TOM Trouble is, she set everyone else off laughing as well...

RUSS Well, it can affect us in different ways. Tears, anger, even laughter occasionally.

TOM Middle of my moving bloody eulogy, taken me hours to write. Stood there feeling like some tatty stand-up comic.

Through the glass, a flash of lightning.

No, the worrying thing is, Russ, the woman's in denial. She refuses to accept the death. She's convinced herself her mother's still alive, you see.

RUSS Still alive?

TOM I think in some way she's blaming herself for the death, you know. I mean it was totally cut and dried. Death by misadventure, coroner's verdict. Straightforward case. Blanche turned her back for a minute, her mother slipped down in the bath, death by drowning. Pure and simple. Poor woman hadn't the strength to pull herself up again.

RUSS Blanche can't blame herself for that, surely? Turning her back for two minutes. She has no reason to blame herself.

TOM Well, she does. What's more she's refusing to accept it even happened.

RUSS Have you talked to her?

TOM She won't listen to me. She needs to talk to...an expert... someone who she trusts. I think Blanche trusts you, Russ.

RUSS I think this may be more of a clinical condition, Tom. It may be a little outside my remit, you know. I think you need a good psychiatrist to get to the bottom of...

A loud rumble of thunder.

BLANCHE, *a woman in her forties, appears from the house, clutching a book.*

BLANCHE Russ!

RUSS Ah! Hallo, Blanche –

BLANCHE What a lovely surprise! What brings you here?

RUSS I was passing – I thought I'd look in on you both. See how you both were.

BLANCHE I didn't hear the doorbell.

RUSS No, your father let me in. He saw me, through the window there and – luckily he let me in.

TOM Just saw him there through the window...

BLANCHE Lucky he did, in this weather...

TOM Luckily for him.

RUSS Luckily for me.

They laugh.

BLANCHE Sorry, I never heard the bell. I was only just upstairs. I usually hear it up there. How are you, Russ?

RUSS Oh, fine. Very well, thank you.

BLANCHE Haven't seen you for ages, have we?

RUSS No. Not since the – Couple of months now. How are you, Blanche?

BLANCHE Me? Oh, busy as ever. I've just been reading to Mother.

A pause.

RUSS Ah!

TOM *clears his throat.*

BLANCHE It's our nightly ritual. She loves it. I've been reading her my new book. Look! *(Holding up the book)* Smart, isn't it?

TOM *(to* RUSS, *in an undertone)* You see what I mean?

RUSS Yes. You've been reading to your mother then, Blanche? That's good.

BLANCHE Mind you, I don't know how much of it she really takes in these days, but I think she finds the sound of my voice soothing. It helps her to sleep a little. Any sleep she gets these days is a blessing.

RUSS Oh yes, sleep. It's a great... Something.

BLANCHE She has such restless nights, poor darling. She's in such discomfort. Ringing her bell, all hours of the night...

RUSS Oh, dear. Yes. That must be a...that must be a...

TOM *(moving to the door of the house)* Russ, old boy. I'll leave you to chat to Blanche, if you don't mind.

RUSS Oh, yes?

TOM I have one or two things to – attend to – in the study. Bills to pay and so on...

RUSS No, really there's no need to rush away, Tom, really –

TOM Nice to have chatted to you, old boy. Cheerio!

TOM *goes out.*

A slight pause. **RUSS** *smiles at* **BLANCHE.** *She smiles back at him.*

BLANCHE Well. How lovely to see you, Russ.

RUSS Lovely to see you, too, Blanche.

BLANCHE I though you must have forgotten about me. You've been such a stranger recently. I don't know why we're standing out here in the damp. We have plenty of drier rooms to choose from. Also warmer. A little bit anyway. Well, as warm as this wretched house ever gets in winter. The only warm place is Mother's room. She's hogging all the fan heaters, as usual.

RUSS *(laughing nervously)* Really? Oh, does she now?

BLANCHE We could sit up there with her, if you like...?

RUSS No, no, no. Here's fine.

BLANCHE She'd love to see you.

RUSS No, no, please. Honestly. This is fine, Blanche. I only popped in to...see how you...both were coping since the – the event we were all at a couple of months ago.

BLANCHE Event? What event?

RUSS Oh – er – it's slipped my mind now... I recall it was great fun. I remember we had a few laughs at the time.

BLANCHE Did we? I can't recall that. When could that have been, I wonder?

RUSS *(coming to a decision)* Blanche. I have something to say to you. Something important I need to talk to you about. Please, sit down.

BLANCHE *(sitting)* Something important? How intriguing! What can that be?

RUSS *(sitting near her)* Now – you have to listen to me very carefully. It's about your mother. Two months ago, Blanche, two months ago –

BLANCHE Oh, just look at the condition of this wretched roof – honestly –

RUSS – two months ago, Blanche –

BLANCHE – would you just look at the state of it –

RUSS – two months ago –

BLANCHE We really must get someone round to look at it –

RUSS Blanche! Please!

BLANCHE – heaven knows what it will cost even getting someone in to look at it!

RUSS *(loudly)* Blanche, will you listen to me, please!

BLANCHE What's that?

RUSS *(hurriedly)* Two months ago, your mother was buried in St Luke's churchyard! Following a simple ceremony which I personally conducted.

BLANCHE *(bemused)* I'm sorry?

RUSS She's dead, Blanche. You have to face it, she is no longer with you. Your mother is deceased. She is no longer with us.

BLANCHE Yes, she is. She's upstairs.

RUSS No, Blanche, she can't be –

BLANCHE I've just this minute finished reading to her –

RUSS No, really, you haven't, Blanche, she's not here. Nonie is no longer here. Your mother is gone, Blanche. You have to face it, she's passed on to a – to a more – to a happier – to somewhere entirely other. Quite probably.

He stops, somewhat confused.

More thunder.

BLANCHE *stares at him.*

Sorry. I can't be of as much help as I could have been once. My faith is — my faith is slightly less – surefooted – than it used to be... Sorry. Anyway she's – she's...your mother's departed, Blanche. She's packed her earthly bags and gone.

BLANCHE She's lying in bed there.

RUSS No...

BLANCHE See for yourself.

RUSS *(alarmed)* What?

BLANCHE Come on! Come with me, I'll show you.

RUSS No, Blanche, she's not up there. She really can't be, you know.

BLANCHE No. On second thoughts, maybe you shouldn't. I've only just got her to sleep.

RUSS *(relieved)* Yes. It would be a shame to...disturb her... wouldn't it?

BLANCHE She'd love to see you sometime, though, Russ. I tell her all about you, you know. She often asks after you.

RUSS Oh, that's nice.

BLANCHE She's looking so much better today. Got some of her old colour back.

RUSS That's the spirit, eh?

An awkward pause.

BLANCHE *fiddles with the book she is still holding.*

(brightly) So. What's that you're reading?

BLANCHE *(handing it to him)* Oh. It's just my latest. That's all.

RUSS *(studying the back of the dust jacket, reading)* Oh, my word, look at these reviews. 'An astonishing tour de force.

The brilliant Blanche Holgate triumphs yet again!' So it's actually been reviewed, has it?

BLANCHE No, those are for an earlier book. They always put those on. Careful with it, won't you, that's my only copy.

RUSS *(putting the book down)* This is the only one?

BLANCHE It's a proof copy. There are others on the way.

RUSS How many?

BLANCHE Oh, only about a dozen. Self publishing is rather expensive.

RUSS So what happens to the other copies?

BLANCHE *(shrugging)* Oh. They'll probably fester down in the cellar there, along with all my other books, still in their boxes. Gathering mould down there.

RUSS How many have you written now?

BLANCHE Fourteen. That's my fifteenth.

RUSS Good lord! I'd have thought with reviews like these...

He breaks off.

Ah! You wrote those as well? The reviews? Well, if you're going to do it yourself, you might as well go the whole hog, mightn't you? Pat yourself firmly on the back? Blanche, getting back to your mother –

BLANCHE I want you to pay special attention to pages one-seven-three to one-seven-four, Russ. They're near the end.

RUSS I certainly will. One-seven-three to one-seven-four... Certainly will. Listen, why don't you try sending them to a few publishers – some of your earlier ones? You never know. There may be one that they pick up on – you never know –

BLANCHE Oh, no. They're rubbish, Russ. All my books are complete rubbish. I sit there by the bed reading aloud to her and I'm blushing with embarrassment. I'm thinking, oh God, another pathetic, empty cliché, or there's another split infinitive...and the terrible thing is, Russ, fifteen books and I've never got the slightest bit better.

RUSS Well, I'm sure even Dickens split the occasional infinitive. There always needs to be hope though, Blanche. You mustn't give up. I know how it feels, I really do. That loss of hope. *(After a pause)* I – er – I don't often talk about this but – years ago I fell in love with someone who... It was a childhood romance, really – I tell myself sometimes that's all it was – she and I, we'd probably have never... I've lost all touch with her these days...no idea where she...who she...even if she... But I've never really lost hope, you see. That one day, quite by chance, we'd both... In my wildest imaginings, all of a sudden she'll walk in through that door. It's sometimes hard – keeping your dreams alive, isn't it? I know only too well. Coping – with real life is so...isn't it? It can be. I do understand. Sometimes it's hard to face. Facts! Horrid things facts. Occasionally. That's what they kept on telling us though, isn't it? When we were children? Learn your facts! They're vitally important, kids! Come along, you need to face facts! Yes. Suffocating.

A pause. BLANCHE *seems very withdrawn.*

When I was a kid, you know, I built this model theatre. Wood, Meccano, I can't remember. A fully operational model theatre. Under stage trap doors, a practical flying system. Spent weeks on it. All through the holidays. Father was furious. Wasting time on frivolities. He made me throw it away.

BLANCHE What was your father, I forget?

RUSS He was a bishop. A rather stern bishop.

BLANCHE I thought all bishops were a bit stern.

RUSS Oh, no. There are one or two jolly bishops, too. These days, they need to be. I know some very jolly ones. It's just that I seem to get lumbered with a stern one as a father. For my sins.

He seems to be the withdrawn one now.

BLANCHE *smiles. She picks up the book from where* **RUSS**
has left it.

Another clap of thunder.

BLANCHE Heavens! What a storm! I hope it doesn't wake
Mother. I must listen out for her.

RUSS Yes.

BLANCHE She's got her bell, mind you. She'll ring if she needs
me. We'll hear her bell ring in here.

RUSS *looks nervously at the bucket.*

I've got them dotted all over the house, you know.

RUSS Yes. So I gathered.

BLANCHE Just in case. I have this nightmare, I'll be somewhere
remote and she'll ring and I won't hear her. In the cellar
or some place.

RUSS What is that then? Another thriller, is it? It is thrillers
you write, isn't it?

BLANCHE Yes. Normally. This latest one's a bit of a departure.
It's still a thriller. Only this time it's a real life crime. It's
something that actually happened, you see.

RUSS Oh, right. I see. A sort of documentary, then?

BLANCHE If you like. It's slightly more autobiographical. Nearer
to home.

RUSS Ah. A real life crime?

BLANCHE Oh, yes. Very, very real.

RUSS Is it – er...? Is it...is it? What sort of crime, is it? Dare
I ask?

BLANCHE Murder, of course.

RUSS Oh, yes. I might have guessed. Good old murder. Nothing like old fashioned murder for shifting a few copies, eh? Especially around Christmas time.

BLANCHE Cold blooded murder, Russ.

RUSS Well, I must remember to buy a copy next time I'm passing a bookshop.

BLANCHE Here! You can have this copy.

RUSS Oh, no, no, no. I couldn't possibly...

BLANCHE Here, take it! I want you to have it, Russ. Take it!

RUSS No, please, it's your – mother's copy, please, I couldn't, really!

BLANCHE *(fiercely)* Take it!

RUSS *(taking it)* Oh, well if you insist. Thank you so much, I'll read it from cover to cover.

BLANCHE I need you to do that, Russ. Every word of it. Every single word. Promise?

RUSS Oh, yes. Promise. I won't skip a syllable. I will indeed. I can't wait to find out who...did it.

BLANCHE I want to know whether you find it authentic. You know, with a murder, it needs to be authentic.

RUSS Oh, yes. Most important.

BLANCHE When you – when a murderer – drowns someone. It needs to be real. To convince the reader it's actually happening.

RUSS Drowns them?

BLANCHE Holds them under the water. Even the frailest of people... The old ones you don't expect to have any strength left at all...not an ounce of strength left in their feeble little atrophied bodies...even they put up a struggle, you know... you'd never expect that, would you?

RUSS *(nervously)* Good heavens, no!

BLANCHE You know another interesting thing. When you're there...holding them down under the water...it takes ages and ages...it seems to go on for ever...at least with my murder, it does...when you read it...it goes on for ever...

RUSS This'll be pages...

BLANCHE ...pages one-seven-three to one-seven-four...

RUSS *(with her)* ...to one-seven-four... Yes.

BLANCHE You think they'll never give up...never die...clinging on... Like they know where they're going...where you're sending them...and they don't want to go...

RUSS Yes...yes...

BLANCHE And here's the oddest thing, Russ. The oddest thing of all. Did you know that even though they're underwater, you're holding their shoulders, pushing down on them, so they're underwater...they're still able to scream...you can still hear them scream...on and on...endlessly...even over the other sounds of their wet, struggling body wriggling, against the bath enamel, crying out, squeaking and squirming...you can still hear their scream...

The book drops on the floor out of RUSS's *fingers.*

RUSS *(horrified)* Oh, dear God! *(Rising and retreating)* I must... I must...excuse me, I must get some...excuse me...

He hurries out into the garden.

BLANCHE But it's still pouring with... *(Rising)* Russ! Don't forget your book...

She goes to the garden door and stares into the night for a moment.

Oh dear! He'll be soaked to the skin, poor thing...

Another rumble of thunder.

After a second, believing she hears something from within the house, she crosses to the other door and listens.

Reassured, she crosses back into the room and picks up the book, which she strokes gently and affectionately.

She glances round the room again, catching sight of the bucket and the submerged bell at the bottom. Puzzled she puts her hand cautiously into the water in order to retrieve it.

Suddenly the bell in her hand starts to ring intermittently and urgently. Startled, she drops it back into the bucket. As it continues to ring, the sound it makes begins to resemble the high pitched underwater scream of a woman's voice.

BLANCHE *stares at it in horror.*

And then to these eerie sounds, she adds a scream of her own.

As she continues to stand there, the lights fade to a: -.

Blackout.

THE POLITICIAN

CHARACTERS

LEO AXMINSTER MP – 40s
BLANCHE HOLGATE – his part time assistant, 40s
ROZ PERKINS – a schoolgirl, 16
SEAN MCKINTYRE – a journalist, 30s
MRS KUYPER – a constituent, 70s

Scene: Leo's constituency office.

LEO's *private constituency inner office at his party's local town centre HQ.*

A desk with a swivel chair. A table alongside piled with files and other paperwork. A sofa with coffee table and an easy chair make an informal area. An upright chair for more formal interviews facing across the desk. Another near the door leading to the outer secretary's office.

Another door to **LEO**'s *private bathroom.*

LEO, *in his forties, in full evening dress, sits at his desk. He is currently in full flow and at his most charming with* **MRS KUYPER,** *a constituent whom he can't wait to get rid of.*

LEO ...no, I say again your point is fully taken, Mrs Kipper. And I'm in total sympathy with you. You have my complete understanding...

MRS K Well, yes, I –

LEO And I do promise you, next Monday morning, as soon as I'm back in Westminster, my feet under my desk, at the first opportunity, I shall button-hole the Minister in person.

MRS K Well no, I –

LEO Because I do know he too is deeply concerned by this problem. And I have his ear, Mrs Kipper, I do have the Transport Minister's ear. And I know for certain this is right at the very top of his agenda, this increasing problem of potholes.

MRS K Well, yes, as I say –

LEO And it's a fact, as you say, that they're on the increase. It's by no means confined to your own back alley, Mrs Kipper, I assure you. But technically, of course, it's a problem for local government, you see...

MRS K Yes, I appreciate –

LEO ...and, to be fair, they have had their hands tied, too. They've been forced to make cut-backs due to the restrictions placed upon them by the Treasury. Which I have to say, in turn, has been entirely brought about by years of neglect by the previous government.

MRS K Yes, well, as I say –

LEO But I do give you my solemn word, Mrs Kipper, that the problem posed by potholes is never far from this government's mind. Particularly when it involves pensioners like yourself –

The intercom on his desk buzzes.

(as he goes to answer) Listen! May I ask you to leave this with me, Mrs Kipper. I promise I'll get back to you, if I haven't had a satisfactory answer by the end of the week, I promise – *(Into phone)* What's that? ...Oh, are they? Are they? Thank you, Blanche – *(Moving to the door)* Listen, I'm so sorry, you'll have to excuse me, Mrs Kipper, I have this local film crew outside, clamouring for an interview – it's all go here – never seems to let up, even at weekends – *(Calling out of the door)* Blanche! Would you mind escorting Mrs Kipper to the lift, if you'd be so kind.

BLANCHE, *in her late forties, his part time local secretary, appears.*

BLANCHE Yes, of course. All finished, have you?

MRS K Yes, I was just saying –

LEO Mrs Kipper and I have been having a right old chin wag, haven't we, Mrs Kipper? *(Wagging a finger at her)* Now, you mind how you go, my dear. Don't go falling down any more of those potholes in the dark now, will you? *(He laughs)*

MRS K Yes. The street lighting, too. It's dreadful...

LEO Cheerio, then! Cheerio!

BLANCHE *(ushering her out)* This way, Mrs Kuyper.

> BLANCHE *and* MRS K *go out. We hear the latter's voice complaining into the distance.* LEO *remains in the doorway, waving her off into the distance until her voice fades and she is finally out of his sight.*

> *On the desk* LEO's *mobile phone rings. He answers it.*

LEO *(into phone)* Yep...no, I'm all finished here, darling... Just got shot of the final one...yep...yep... I've got this last minute TV interview...yes, I know...oh, far less than that...they're just looking for a brief sound bite... Yep, ten minutes at the outside...yep, I'll be there. See you soon, darling. 'Byeee.

> *He rings off as* BLANCHE *returns.*

Thank God. Got shot of that wretched woman at last, have we?

BLANCHE Yes, she's a little – Mrs Kuyper can be a trifle persistent, can't she?

LEO How are you keeping, Blanche? I haven't asked you. How're your parents? Both keeping fit, are they?

BLANCHE Well, my father's a little – his memory's going a little, these days, I'm afraid...

LEO *(not listening heartily)* That's the spirit! Glad to hear it.

BLANCHE ...and my mother is still bedridden, of course...

LEO Splendid! Splendid! That's excellent news!

BLANCHE Yes.

LEO What name did you call that woman?

BLANCHE Sorry?

LEO That woman, what did you call her just now?

BLANCHE Who, Mrs Kuyper?

LEO Mrs <u>Kuyper</u>. Is that her name?

BLANCHE Yes.

LEO God, I've been calling her Kipper.

BLANCHE I know you have.

LEO Why the hell didn't you correct me then, Blanche?

BLANCHE I do. I do tell you every time she comes to see you. You never listen, Leo.

LEO Kuyper? What sort of a name is Kuyper?

BLANCHE I think it's possibly Dutch originally.

LEO Dutch? You don't mean she's foreign? What's the point of my wasting time with her if she doesn't even vote?

BLANCHE No, I think she's a local.

LEO Where's this film crew? Are they here?

BLANCHE They're next door. Waiting in the pub.

LEO Well, what are they doing in the pub? Why aren't they here? I have this charity dinner I need to be at. I can't be late for that... If I'm late for that, Marjory's going to be livid. She keeps phoning me every five minutes as it is...

BLANCHE I don't blame her. She has a point. You're invariably late.

LEO Me?

BLANCHE You're never on time. It must be infuriating being married to you. She has my every sympathy, poor woman.

LEO Oh, don't you start... *(Angrily)* Where's this bloody film crew, then? Where the hell are they? I'm ready. I'm not the one who's late, now, am I?

The bell to the outer office door rings.

BLANCHE *(as she goes)* Alright, calm down, calm down! That'll be them, now.

BLANCHE *goes out briefly.*

LEO Half of them rolling drunk. God, how I loathe and despise journalists!

LEO *takes one or two deep breaths and practices his smile, preparing himself.*

BLANCHE *returns alone.*

(with his charming smile) Ah, come in! Do come in, chaps! Make yourselves – *(He breaks off)* Well, where are they?

BLANCHE It wasn't them.

LEO Who was it? Not another bloody whingeing Dutch constituent, surely?

BLANCHE *(frowning)* No. It's one of your – nieces...

LEO Nieces?

BLANCHE *(distastefully)* One of your so-called – I don't know – whatever you choose to call them. She says her name is Rose or Roz or something.

LEO Rose? I don't know any Rose.

BLANCHE No, I don't think she's one of your regulars.

LEO Oh, my God! Where is she?

BLANCHE Just outside. I left her waiting by my desk.

LEO Well, get rid of her, Blanche! At once!

BLANCHE You want me to send her away?

LEO Of course send her away. I can't see her now, can I? I've got a film crew due here imminently, followed by a Save the Countryside Charity Dinner, for Christ's sake! What were you thinking of, woman? I didn't book her. We can't have her here with a bloody film crew, can we?

BLANCHE I'm afraid your private life has nothing to do with me, Leo. She wasn't in your diary, so I booked the film crew.

LEO Of course she wasn't in my diary. Now, get rid of her at once!

The front door bell rings again. They freeze.

BLANCHE Film crew.

LEO How are we going to explain her?

BLANCHE I'll – say she's your niece. Tell them she's just leaving.

LEO Not in front of a journalist, woman. They'll be on to her immediately. They've got minds like open sewers, that lot.

BLANCHE Well, what else do you want me to say?

LEO What's she look like? Is she reasonably presentable?

BLANCHE Yes, she's reasonable enough. Very young.

LEO How young?

BLANCHE I think she's got a school uniform on.

LEO Oh, my God. Bring her in here! Bring her in here, then!

BLANCHE In here?

The doorbell rings again.

LEO We'll have to keep her in here till they've gone.

BLANCHE Where are you going to do the interview?

LEO I'll do it out there.

BLANCHE Out there?

LEO Sitting at your little desk. It'll look – it'll make me look more – humble. Bring the girl in here. You can stay and keep an eye on her. There's a lot of highly confidential stuff lying about in here. We don't want her going through it with her grimy little teenage fingers, do we?

BLANCHE We could always get her to hide in the bathroom there.

LEO What, with a film crew full of beer bursting for a pee? What are they going to think if they find a bloody schoolgirl in my bathroom?

The doorbell rings again.

Now for goodness' sake, Blanche, fetch her in here and then open the door to them!

BLANCHE Right. *(As she goes)* I have to say this is getting most complicated.

BLANCHE *goes out briefly. She returns pushing* **ROZ**, *a girl of sixteen, ahead of her.* **ROZ** *is wearing her school uniform under her coat.*

This way. Here she is. This is – Rose. Excuse me a moment.

BLANCHE *goes straight out again.*

LEO *(brusquely)* Come in, girl! Come in, then!

ROZ Your doorbell kept ringing. I didn't know whether to answer it?

LEO No. Certainly not. *(Indicating the sofa)* Now sit there and don't bloody move.

ROZ *(unfazed by his attitude)* Thank you. This your office then, is it?

LEO Yes.

ROZ Big, isn't it?

LEO Don't you dare touch anything, either.

Silence.

ROZ What do we do now, then? Want to see my pictures, do you?

LEO *(suspiciously)* Pictures? What pictures?

ROZ My ten by eights.

LEO Pictures of what?

ROZ Pictures of me. Head shots mostly. There's one or two full length but I wasn't sure if they were relevant. My agent told me to bring them in case.

LEO Your agent? You have an agent?

ROZ Gale Devonne. Force Ten Promotions.

BLANCHE *returns.*

BLANCHE *(discreetly)* The – film crew – are just setting up, Mr Axminster. They're nearly ready for you.

LEO Oh, right. Thank you, Blanche. Keep an eye on Rose here.

LEO *goes out.*

ROZ Film crew?

BLANCHE *(tight-lipped)* Yes. *(She sits on a chair near the door)*

ROZ Didn't know there was going to be a film crew. Like a sort of camera test this, is it? Only I'd have done my eyes better if I'd known. Done them properly.

BLANCHE They're not here to film you, young woman. As far as they're concerned, you're not here at all. They're only interested in Mr Axminster.

ROZ Right.

Slight pause.

What's he doing, then? Like a kind of sort of documentary, is it?

BLANCHE *(coolly)* I've no idea what he's doing.

ROZ Right.

Slight pause.

You don't work here, then?

BLANCHE Of course I do. I'm his secretary.

ROZ *(seemingly unconvinced)* Ah.

BLANCHE I certainly do work here. Very hard indeed. Whenever Mr Axminster's here. Whenever he chooses to be here. On the increasingly rare occasions of late when he deigns to be here.

ROZ Only with you being his secretary I'd have thought you'd have known what he was up to.

BLANCHE What?

ROZ You said just now you had no idea what he was doing. Which means either he's not telling you or else he's told you and you've not been paying attention.

BLANCHE He – I – No. I meant, if I did know. What he's doing. Which I do know, as it happens. If you must know. Then I certainly wouldn't tell you. It's nothing whatever to do with you. It's none of your business.

ROZ Well. *(Cheerfully)* That's me told then, isn't it?

On the desk, LEO's mobile rings.

They look at it.

It rings again.

BLANCHE, with a glance towards the door, decides to answer it.

BLANCHE I'd better answer this. It'll disturb the filming. *(Answering)* Hallo, Mr Axminster's mobile...oh, hallo, Mrs Axminster...no, he's in mid-interview at present with the BBC ...yes... *(With a look towards ROZ)* ...yes... I see... *(Covering the phone briefly, to ROZ, hissing)* Wait there! Do not move one inch! ... *(Resuming the call)* ...yes...sorry, Mrs Axminster...say again...

BLANCHE steps into the bathroom briefly to continue the call.

ROZ *sits alone on the sofa. In a moment her own phone rings. Alarmed, she swiftly retrieves it from her bag, briefly studies the screen and then decides to answer it.*

ROZ Tracy, hi! ...No... I'm at this audition... No, an acting audition. No, my agent sent me... No, not Rev Russ... No, Gale... Gale Devonne, my new agent... She's brilliant. You should see her list of clients, Trace. Everyone from Chuck Norris... Yeah. She sent me along...no, I'm just waiting in his office...he's this big producer, apparently, though I think he's into other things as well, like politics and stuff...yes... listen, Trace, I can't talk now...this old cow's just outside the door...yes, right...see you in the pub later...yeah...

Under this, BLANCHE *returns from the bathroom.*

BLANCHE *(as she re-enters, into phone)* ...yes, I'll be sure to tell him. 'Bye.

She switches off her phone with a beep. A split second later ROZ *does likewise. She hastily returns her phone to her bag.*

BLANCHE *looks at* ROZ *suspiciously.*

What are you doing?

ROZ Pardon?

BLANCHE Just then? What were you doing?

ROZ Nothing.

BLANCHE *(suspiciously, returning* LEO*'s phone to the desk)* Yes.

She decides to sit behind the desk to assert authority. She seems impatient to get away. She looks at her watch. Straightens the already straight desk. She drums her fingers and looks at her watch again.

ROZ *watches her.*

ROZ Actually, I'm a bit nervous. I never done one of these before.

BLANCHE You haven't?

ROZ This is my first one.

BLANCHE My God! How old are you?

ROZ Sixteen.

BLANCHE *(closing her eyes)* Dear heaven!

ROZ I'll be seventeen next month.

BLANCHE What sort of world are we living in? What a world we've created for ourselves!

ROZ You think I look too old?

BLANCHE Too old?

ROZ I can look younger. If I don't wear any make up at all, I can look about twelve. I heard he's looking for young schoolgirl types. I wasn't sure how young he wanted them to be. My agent didn't say. Only I thought I'd wear my uniform, you see. My school uniform. I thought it might help. *(Rising to remove her coat)* Look, I'll show you –

BLANCHE *(shrilly)* Don't take it off!

ROZ *(startled in mid-action)* What?

BLANCHE Not in front of me, if you don't mind. Now, put it on! Put that on again, at once!

ROZ *(puzzled)* Right.

BLANCHE *(more quietly)* I have no wish to see – any of that. Sort of thing.

SEAN, *an interviewer, appears briefly in the doorway.*

SEAN Sorry, could we keep the noise down a bit, please?

BLANCHE So sorry.

SEAN Just while we're recording. *(Smiling at them both)* Won't be too much longer, I promise.

SEAN *takes another brief glance at* ROZ *and goes off again.*

A slight pause.

ROZ You got a thing about them then, have you? School uniforms? Like a phobia, is it?

BLANCHE Not at all. What are you talking about?

ROZ Only my younger sister's got a phobia. About men with beards. Man with a beard comes near her and she goes all cold, all pale and she starts sweating, you know. It's always dead miserable for her at Christmas. *(Laughing)* I said to her, Fran, it's a good job you're not a Muslim, girl! Beards everywhere then, eh?

Silence. BLANCHE *is stony faced.*

Sorry. It's just I'm getting really nervous now. Moved on from nearly pissing myself to shit scared. Sorry. You're not a Muslim, are you?

BLANCHE Certainly not.

ROZ No, you don't look like a Muslim.

BLANCHE I'm strictly Church of England.

ROZ Yes, you look more strictly Church of England. *(Slight pause)* Is he going to be much longer, do you think?

BLANCHE You heard what he said. Not long. *(With another glance at her watch)* I hope.

ROZ *hunches up, her nerves beginning to get to her.*

ROZ Ooooh! Terrible. I'm beginning to feel sick now.

BLANCHE *(slightly alarmed)* Sick?

ROZ It's just the waiting. I'd wound myself up to do it, you know, got myself all prepared. I thought I'd just come in here and do it straightaway, you know. I didn't realise there was going to be this wait. Only with me, you know, I need to get myself worked up first. In the mood, you know. But then I'm only starting out, you see. I expect if I was more experienced, if I was a professional, I'm sure I wouldn't have this trouble. My teacher, the man who teaches me, he taught me everything I know really, I owe it all to him. He always tells me, don't peak before you're ready, girl. You have to feel it first – in here. See? If you don't feel it for yourself, how do you expect anyone else to feel it? He's brilliant. I love him. He's a really good man, he is. He's a vicar.

BLANCHE *has been listening to this with growing horror. Her head now slumps on to the desk. She makes little whimpering sounds.*

I think he's Church of England like you, actually. You alright there, are you?

BLANCHE *(breathing heavily, rising)* I'm sorry, I can't take any more of this! *(Loudly)* I simply can't take any more!

She rushes back into the bathroom.

ROZ *(calling after her)* Sorry. Have I upset you again? *(To herself)* She's really weird, she is!

SEAN *appears briefly in the doorway again.*

SEAN *(finger to his lips)* Sorry, just a couple more minutes. Be patient.

ROZ Yes. Sorry – *(Indicating* BLANCHE*)* – she's – she's just gone in the –

SEAN *has gone back off.*

ROZ *walks up and down to work off her nerves. She starts shallow breathing, hands on her hips, breathing from her diaphragm.*

BLANCHE *returns, still looking shaky. She stops in the doorway as she sees* ROZ.

ROZ, *conscious of having to keep the noise down, now starts silent mouth stretching exercises. She flaps her tongue.*

(*aware of* BLANCHE, *quietly*) Just getting my mouth working properly.

BLANCHE (*nervously edging away*) Yes. You do that, dear.

ROZ Listen, tell you what, while we're waiting – can I do a bit for you – would you mind?

BLANCHE What?

ROZ Just a little bit – while I'm in the mood? Would you mind?

BLANCHE (*shaking her head, softly*) No, no...please. No.

ROZ (*making up her mind*) Yes, go on, I'll give you a little bit, why not? I'll give you a little taste of *The Seagull*, a little bit of *Seagull*, shall I? You fancy a bit of *Seagull*?

ROZ *removes her coat which she tosses on to the sofa.*

BLANCHE (*edging to the door, terrified*) Seagull? What's the seagull? What are you going to do to me?

ROZ Sssshhh! I can't do it very loud though. Shhh!

ROZ *advances, Chekhovian madness blazing in her eyes, on the hapless* BLANCHE, *who stands rigid with fear, her back to the door.*

(*directly to* BLANCHE, *in a hoarse whisper*) "Somebody ought to kill me. I'm so tired. If only I could rest! Rest! I am a seagull..." (*She makes a sharp seagull noise*)

BLANCHE *screams, turns and finally rushes out of the door.*

ROZ *remains in the room, a little surprised at the effect her performance has had on her audience of one.*

From outside, the sound of raised voices. Amongst them: –.

SEAN *(offstage)* Cut! Cut! Cut it!

LEO *(offstage)* Oh, for God's sake! Blanche! Pull yourself together! What's got into you, woman? *(Calling after her)* Blanche, come back here! Blanche!

In a moment, **LEO** *enters.*

(angrily) What the hell's been going on in here? Was that your doing?

ROZ No.

LEO What did you do to her? What the hell did you do to my secretary?

ROZ *(indignantly)* Nothing. I didn't do nothing! She's truly weird!

SEAN *attempts to enter behind* **LEO** *who is blocking the doorway.*

SEAN *(as he attempts to enter)* That's fine, thank you, Leo. We've got enough.

LEO *(turning)* Don't come in! Don't come in here!

In panic, he pushes **SEAN** *back out again.*

SEAN *(offstage)* No, I'm just saying, Leo, not to worry. We've got more than enough there –

LEO *(back blocking the doorway)* Jolly good. Jolly good – Stan. Glad to hear it.

SEAN *(offstage)* Sean. It's Sean. Thanks very much! We'll be off then.

LEO *(calling)* Cheerio! Let yourselves out, will you?

SEAN *(offstage)* We will. Thanks again, Leo.

LEO *(calling)* Always happy to talk to the BBC, Stan. Always happy! *(Turning back into the room, muttering)* Bloody rat pack! Scum of the earth! *(Glaring at* **ROZ***)* As for you, the sooner you're out of here the better.

ROZ You want me to go?

LEO Yes!

ROZ You don't want me to do anything for you?

LEO The sooner you're out of here, the better for all of us. Go on, get out.

ROZ *(crushed)* Right.

She gathers up her things and moves to the door. She is angry and disappointed and we suspect is about to cry.

LEO Wait! Not yet!

ROZ *(stopping in the doorway)* What?

LEO Not yet, girl. That lot are still out there, packing up their paraphernalia. Wait till they're clear of the building.

He returns to his desk and picks up his phone. **ROZ** *stands awkwardly waiting, still holding her stuff.*

ROZ You don't want me to do nothing for you?

LEO Nothing.

ROZ Only I came all this way on the bus. Got myself ready and everything. All dressed up. It won't take long, I promise...

LEO What do you mean, it won't take long?

ROZ No, I mean, I can keep it short, if you'd prefer.

LEO I think it's rather up to me how long it takes, isn't it? The amount you lot charg – Oh I get it! I get it. This is what you're after, isn't it? *(Laughing)* I might have guessed it.

LEO *opens a drawer in the desk and brings out a brown envelope which he tosses on to the desk.*

Here! Presumably that's what you're hanging about for, isn't it? Go on, take it! Take it, then! You haven't earned a penny of it! Got me over a bloody barrel though, haven't you? One word from you lot and that's me... Go on, take it before I change my mind!

ROZ *picks up the envelope cautiously.*

It's all there. Count it if you want to.

ROZ You mean I get paid?

LEO What?

ROZ I didn't realise we got paid.

LEO Oh, very funny. What the hell did you expect?

ROZ I suppose I'll need to give some to my agent, won't I?

LEO Presumably you will. Unless you want to end up in hospital. I think he'll probably expect it.

ROZ She.

LEO She, then. *(He looks at his watch)* You're new to this, I take it?

ROZ Yes, it's my first.

LEO What? Your first?

ROZ Yes.

LEO Ever? Your very first?

ROZ Yes.

LEO Oh, my God. How old are you?

ROZ Sixteen –

LEO You sure about that?

ROZ Yes, I'll be seventeen next –

LEO *(torn, then coming to a decision)* Alright. We'll have to make it quick. Come on then –

ROZ *(excitedly)* I can do it then, can I? I can do something for you?

She starts to put her things back on the sofa.

LEO Check the door, first! Make sure they've gone!

ROZ Right.

She looks cautiously through the door.

LEO All clear?

ROZ All clear.

She moves back to the centre of the room and hesitates.
He sits on the desk expectantly.

LEO Come on then, get a move on! What are you waiting for?

ROZ I don't know which of my bits to do first.

LEO My God, you are new to this, aren't you?

ROZ No, you see I've got three.

LEO Three?

ROZ Bits.

LEO *(mystified)* Bits? What bits?

ROZ Well, I've got my introductory bit which is fairly short, a bit of *The Seagull* – and then there's –

LEO A bit of the what?

ROZ *The Seagull*, don't you know it?

LEO No, I've never had that before. Is it good? Will I enjoy it?

ROZ Well, it's a bit sad. Whenever I do it, it generally makes people cry.

LEO Oh, no, I don't fancy that. I'm not into that sort of thing. Anyway, I've got a dinner to go to in a minute... What else have you got?

ROZ I've got my big set piece, that's my own original –

LEO That'll do, that sounds good. Let's have that.

ROZ And then I planned to finish off with a bit of *Much Ado*.

LEO No, skip that. Let's have the big one. Come on, now! We're running out of time, girl... My wife's due here any minute to pick me up.

ROZ Alright.

ROZ fetches her ghetto blaster which she sets down on the floor next to her. She is about to set it off and then hesitates.

No, sorry. I can't just go straight into that. It's impossible. I need to do a little of my first piece. I mean if I go straight in to the other one, I'll lose my timing you see, I'll lose my rhythm –

LEO *(impatiently)* Alright, alright, alright! Do a bit of your first one! Whatever you want!

ROZ It's quite short.

She drops her head, shakes her shoulders loose and takes a breath or two by way of preparation. She starts off on her own highly personal take on Nina. Although the text is far from the original version, ROZ's reading has an intensity and sincerity which might not altogether have displeased the master.

LEO *(raising his eyes to heaven)* Dear God, there's more build up to this than bloody Gypsy Rose Lee –

ROZ "When you next see Trigorin, don't tell him nothing, will you –?"

LEO Who?

ROZ "I love him. I love him more than ever. *(Smiling)* You could write a book about that, couldn't you?" *(She laughs)*

LEO Book about what?

ROZ *(continuing undeterred)* "Yes, of course I love him. I get wet for him every time I think of him. It used to be just brilliant –"

She pauses as if recalling the moment. It's quite a long one.

LEO *(angrily)* Oh for God's sake, woman. Get a bloody move on, will you?

ROZ *(startled)* What?

LEO I don't know about you but I'm in a hurry. So cut all that boring pre-amble and get on with it!

A pause.

ROZ *(quietly)* Right.

LEO's phone chimes as a text message comes through. He checks the screen.

LEO That's my wife. She's on her way now. She'll be here in five minutes.

ROZ *(grimly)* Right.

She is clearly deeply hurt and offended. As she continues with the following, she will give vent to her full anger. It is eventually quite frightening. It clearly scares **LEO**.

(icily) This is my own version of Gilbert and Sullivan's *Three Little Maids From School*, only you haven't got three, you've only got one, this one. So bollocks!

LEO What the hell are you on about now –?

His voice is drowned out as she sets her ghetto blaster off. A loud chord to start her off.

ROZ *(singing, demurely)*
ONE LITTLE GIRL IN SCHOOL, THAT'S ME,
PERT AS A SCHOOL GIRL WELL CAN BE,
FILLED TO THE BRIM WITH GIRLISH GLEE
ONE LITTLE MAID FROM SCHO-OOOL!

A drum and bass track cuts in at volume.

ROZ *rapidly changes her demeanour, becoming angrier and darker.*

(rapping to the beat)
I'M A BITCH! I'M A BITCH! I'M A RED HOT BITCH!

I'M A WITCH! I'M A WITCH! I'M AN ICE COLD WITCH!
I'M HERE TO BE OBEYED AND I'M NO MAN'S MAID.
I'M FIRST IN CLASS AND I'LL WHIP YOUR ARSE...

LEO *(somewhat alarmed)* Oh, my God...!

ROZ *(continuing over him)*
I GOT INTELLECT, SO I NEED RESPECT.
YEAH, I'M NO MAN'S WHORE, I AIN'T NO MAN'S TOY.
IF YOU FUCK WITH ME, THEN I'LL FUCK YOU, BOY.
AND I'LL CUT THEM OFF WITH A BIG SHARP KNIFE,
AND THEN POST THEM BACK TO YOUR SEX-STARVED WIFE!
KEEP YOUR HANDS TITS FREE, DON'T YOU TOUCH MY CUNT,
'COS I DON'T GIVE PUSSY TO THE NATIONAL FRONT!
I'M A BITCH! I'M A BITCH! I'M A DANGEROUS BITCH...

She has advanced on **LEO** *so she is now screaming into his face. Eventually, his nerve breaks and he rushes to the door.*

LEO *(as he goes)* Dear God! She's mad! Help me, someone! She's a mad woman. Somebody, help!

ROZ *(as he goes, reaching the conclusion of her song)* I'm a witch! I'm a witch! I'm an ice cold witch...! *(The big finish)* Fuck yo – o – o – o – u!

The backing tape stops.

A slight pause as **ROZ** *returns to normal.*

(calling after him) Do I get the job?

She listens for a reply. A distant door slams.

(shrugging) Oh.

She gathers up her stuff.

She examines the envelope he has given her.

It is filled with money.

Oh. That's nice.

She packs away the envelope without bothering to count it.

Having assembled her stuff, she moves to the door. As she does so, SEAN *steps into the doorway.*

SEAN Hi! Just came back for a piece of kit – we're always leaving our stuff... Sean McKintyre, BBC local news. Hi!

ROZ BBC? Oh, yes. Did you see which way he went, then? Mr Axminster? Has he left?

SEAN Oh, yes, I think so. He came running past me. Left the main door open. I noticed his wife downstairs, waiting in the car...

ROZ Yes, he said he was in a hurry...

A slight pause.

(making to move past him) Well... I must...

SEAN *(not moving)* Do you mind me asking, have you known him long?

ROZ No. Only just met him, haven't I?

SEAN You're not his niece?

ROZ His what?

SEAN His niece? Someone – told me you were his niece.

ROZ His niece? No. Not at all.

SEAN Right.

ROZ That would make him my uncle then, wouldn't it?

SEAN It would.

ROZ No. Don't think I'd fancy an uncle like him. Wouldn't care for that. I got one that's totally mad, I don't want another.

SEAN Listen, are you in a hurry? Could you spare a minute?

ROZ Well, I was meant to be meeting my friend...

SEAN Just five minutes. There's a good pub next door. Tell you what, let me buy you a drink, courtesy of the BBC. Just a quick word...

ROZ No, I don't mind talking to the BBC. It can maybe help me with my career a bit, couldn't it...? *(She laughs)*

SEAN Yes, I'm sure it could... And you are –? Sorry, I didn't catch your name, I'm afraid?

ROZ Oh, I'm Roz – no, Rose.

SEAN Rose?

ROZ That's my professional name.

SEAN Professional?

ROZ That's what I'm hoping to be. A top professional. I can't wait to get there, either.

SEAN I see. Well, let's talk about that some more, shall we? *(Stepping aside)* After you – Rose.

SEAN *makes to follow her but can't resist turning back into the room at the desk.*

(punching the air with satisfaction, softly) Oh, yes! Got you!

He turns to follow ROZ.

ROZ *(offstage, excitedly)* ...No, my real ambition eventually is to have my own programme, you see. I mean, I don't care what I do really, singing, dancing, bit of acting. I could do like, sketches, you know... I'm especially strong on comedy... I particularly enjoy doing comedy...

Her voice fades into the distance. As they go, music and the lights fade to a: –.

Blackout.

THE STAR

CHARACTERS

RUSS TIMMS – a clergyman, 30s
GALE DEVONNE – an entrepreneur, 30s
ROZ PERKINS – a schoolgirl, 16
MRS MILLER – a choreographer, 40s

Scene: Saturday afternoon in a church hall in a run-down urban area.

A table and two chairs, centrally placed.

At one side, a sofa untidily piled with the coats and outerwear belonging to young performers currently occupying the hall. Strewn about, an inverted armchair and a coffee table both evidently long unfit for purpose; in a corner, a desk with a swivel chair, apparently the dumping centre for schoolbags, etc.

Two exits, one leading to the foyer and beyond that the front doors of the hall leading to the street.

The other is open to what we imagine to be the far end of the hall. It is from here that we hear offstage rehearsal activity which continues intermittently throughout. This consists of a group of enthusiastic, variously talented teenagers engaged in a music rehearsal for a forthcoming production of Gilbert and Sullivan's The Mikado. *They are in the midst of a dance number with piano accompaniment. Sounds of feet and the occasional interruption by the female choreographer.*

This continues for a few seconds till we hear **MRS MILLER,** *the choreographer, as her voice cuts in.*

MRS M *(her frustrated voice, offstage)* No, no, no, no, NO! Stop!

The piano stops abruptly. Various young voices raised in protest and dissent.

Roz! Roz! Where are you going? We're in the middle of a rehearsal here! Roz, come back here at once!

ROZ, a girl of sixteen, stamps on in her practice clothes. As she does so, she flings her script angrily in the direction of the sofa. She pulls up, flushed and panting, partly through physical exhaustion but also in anger and frustration.

RUSS, a clergyman aged about thirty, hurries on after her and stands close to her.

RUSS *(quietly and anxiously)* Roz? Now come on, Roz. You can do it! Roz, come along, now...

ROZ *(quietly, on the verge of tears)* I can't! She's rubbish! She's total <u>crap!</u>

RUSS Roz...

ROZ It's just crap! It just looks totally shit! The whole thing's crap! She doesn't know nothing!

RUSS Roz, now listen! Mrs Miller was a professional choreographer for thirty years –

ROZ Yeah, till they sacked her. Till they kicked her out. Stupid ignorant cow!

RUSS Roz! Now, stop that! Now, you're just being silly!

ROZ I'm not doing this. I'm leaving. I'm not doing this no more...

RUSS Roz, if you walk out now, I warn you –

ROZ All of it's shit! It's stupid and racist. I don't want nothing more to do with it. I'm leaving.

RUSS Roz! Will you calm down, please! Calm down and listen for a minute! Now sit down! *(Firmly)* Sit!

ROZ sits and calms down a little. During the next, RUSS retrieves her script and places it on the table beside her.

Now, we all got together, didn't we, all of us, two months ago, the whole committee – you were there – and we agreed, didn't we, that it was time for something different? We'd done our Shakespeare and we'd done our Chekhov. And we'd

done our – somewhat unfortunate – Pirandello – my fault
entirely that – and we all of us agreed, didn't we? No, be fair,
we all voted to do a musical. Now we're doing a musical –

ROZ *(sulkily)* We didn't mean this sort of musical, did we? We
meant a proper musical.

RUSS What do you mean? *The Mikado* is a proper musical. It's
a classic musical. What else would you call it?

ROZ No it's not, it's opera. Says so on the front of the script.
We wanted to do a proper musical with proper singing and
dancing. No, listen, I don't mind working with you. I enjoy
working with you, Russ, you know I do. I respect you. But
I'm not working with her. I don't mind you telling me things
'cos you usually know what you're talking about. But I'm not
having her shouting and pushing and pulling, breathing all
over me with her horrible bad breath. 'Cos she's crap and I
don't respect her, not at all. Either she goes or I do, right?
Her or me? Get rid of her.

RUSS Now, be sensible. We can't get rid of her. We need a
choreographer.

ROZ Why can't you do it, then?

RUSS Because I'm not a proper choreographer –

ROZ You'd be better than her. I'm saying, I'm not working
with her. I'll work with you – I'll even work with old Ratts
providing he keeps his hands on his keyboard –

RUSS You really are so stubborn, Roz, sometimes, aren't you?
Sometimes you can be...your own worst enemy. I mean,
last month, jumping down off the stage in the middle of
the Chekhov and punching a member of the audience...

ROZ She kept opening her fucking sweets right through my
big speech! She deserved a slapping, didn't she? It was
disrespectful – to me!

RUSS Roz, you have real talent. I keep telling you that. You have
the makings of something – so exciting and remarkable.

You're capable of creating such – beauty onstage. But there's also this part of you that simply wants to kick it all to pieces. Don't walk away again, Roz. Please. You know how important you are to us. You know that.

ROZ Yes, I know that.

RUSS You've got a great future.

ROZ If I'm given a chance, I have! Otherwise, I'll probably end up like my mum, won't I? With five kids. Playing the clubs.

RUSS Is that what she does? Your mother? I didn't know that.

ROZ Yes. She's retired now.

RUSS I never knew that. What was she, a singer?

ROZ No, she was a – an exotic dancer down at Mustard's Club. Used to be.

RUSS How exciting!

ROZ She used to do an act with this snake.

RUSS Oh, I see. That sort of exotic.

ROZ Till they took it away from her.

RUSS Took it away? Who took it away?

ROZ The sodding council, didn't they? Said she was endangering the health of the animal.

RUSS Good gracious!

ROZ They come and took it off her. Middle of her performance. In the middle of Mustard's, marched in and took it off her. Typical. No one worried about my mum's welfare, did they? About her livelihood? Didn't matter about her, it was all about this fucking stupid snake, wasn't it? Typical!

Slight pause.

No, I'll probably end up like her. Follow the family tradition.

RUSS *(smiling)* Won't you need a snake first?

ROZ *(scowling at his feeble joke)* Look, I'm going home now.

RUSS Roz, you can't! You mustn't throw it all away. Not now we've put in your drama school applications. We've raised most of the money –

ROZ You have, you mean.

RUSS No. We all have. We've raised it together. Most of it. You can't disappoint us now, let us all down. Not just because of her, Mrs Miller. She's not worth it, surely? Giving it all up simply because of her?

A slight pause. Rehearsals at the other end of the hall appear to have stopped temporarily. There is a murmur of voices.

Ah, they've stopped rehearsing. We appear to be taking a break. Now, why don't you grab this opportunity to go back and apologise to Mrs Miller?

Silence.

Please, Roz. For me. For yourself. You'll feel better.

ROZ No. Not till she apologises to me first. She has to know, she can't just grab hold of people like that. Invading their personal space...

RUSS Well, I'll have a word with Mrs Miller. Ask her to be less... invasive... Wait there. Oh dear, you never make things easy do you, Roz? You really are... Sometimes. Just wait there. Please. Promise you won't rush off again like you did last week. You have to promise me!

ROZ Right. Promise.

RUSS goes off, shaking his head.

RUSS *(calling as he goes)* Mrs Miller, may I have a quick word with you? In the office, please?

MRS M *(offstage)* Yes, of course, Russell... Has the girl calmed down now? I hope she has...

ROZ *(half to herself)* Stupid old cow...

> ROZ *continues to watch the proceedings. She appears
> unperturbed by the disruption she has caused. She picks
> up her script.*

> *As she sits there,* GALE, *aged about thirty, elegant and
> smartly dressed, enters through the front door. She
> hesitates and sees* ROZ.

GALE *(calling tentatively)* Excuse me... I say, excuse me.

> ROZ, *glaring at her script, looks up.*

You wouldn't by any chance be Roz, would you? Roz Perkins?

ROZ *(guardedly)* I might be.

GALE Yes, I thought you might be. Hi, I'm Gale. Gale Devonne.

> ROZ *looks blank.*

We spoke on the phone. You called me a couple of days ago.
Force Ten Promotions.

ROZ Oh, yes, right. You're the agent.

GALE *(smiling)* Gale Devonne. Hi. *(She extends a hand)*

ROZ *(accepting it)* Hi.

GALE Mind if I sit down?

ROZ *(without moving)* Help yourself.

GALE Not interrupting anything, am I? Only I saw the sign on
the door there. I take it you're still rehearsing?

ROZ No. We're on a break.

GALE Right. Incidentally, would you mind telling me how you
got in touch with me?

ROZ Someone gave me your number. I thought I needed an
agent, so I called you.

GALE Where did you get it? My number?

ROZ Friend of my mother's. She recommended you. Lindy. Lindy Kuze.

GALE Oh, Lindy.

ROZ You know Lindy, do you?

GALE *(offhand)* Yes. Slightly. *(Noticing the script)* Is this what you're rehearsing then, is it? *The Mikado*? That's fun. What are you playing?

ROZ *(through clenched teeth)* Yum-Yum. I'm playing Yum-Yum.

GALE Oh, that's a great part! *Three Little Maids From School Are We...*

ROZ Yeah, I'm changing the name.

GALE Changing it?

ROZ I'm not having my mates in the audience taking the piss, I can tell you.

GALE Well, once you get into the spirit of it, I'm sure you'll find it'll be great fun.

ROZ That's what Russ keeps telling us.

GALE Who?

ROZ The director. He keeps going on about us having fun. Have fun, that's what he keeps saying...

GALE You're not having fun, I take it?

ROZ It's rubbish.

GALE You think so? I remember doing *The Mikado* when I was at school. Went down a storm with the juniors. But then – it was...well, circumstances were a bit different.

ROZ A bit different to here, you mean? At your school?

GALE A little.

ROZ *(dryly)* Yes, I thought it might be. You done acting, then?

GALE Oh, yes. In the old days. Given up now.

ROZ You didn't enjoy it?

GALE I wasn't very good. If you're not very good in this business,
darling, if you have any sense, you get out when you're
young. Before it finally throws you out in middle age. You
enjoy it then, do you? Acting?

ROZ Yes. It's amazing. I was no good at anything before – At
home, all my sisters, my brother, early on, they started being
good at all different things, you know – cooking or drawing
or sports – nicking cars. Me? I couldn't do nothing. At school
I was bottom of everything. Then when I left, I joined here,
you know... Didn't really want to – this friend of mine told
me about it – I think she had a thing about the director,
you know – about Russ. But then I got this small part, you
know, just a couple of lines...but as soon as I was on the
stage, I knew... I just knew...

GALE You knew this was something you could do...

ROZ No, I knew I was going to be brilliant. I knew one day,
I was going to be a star. No one could stop me, you see...

GALE (smiling) Yes, well, all of us, we tend to...

ROZ No. Seriously. I'm going to be star. A real star. I'm positive
of that. If I don't know nothing else, I'm certain of it. I'll
be right up there at the very top.

GALE Acting?

ROZ Acting, singing, dancing. I can do them all. I'm a brilliant
dancer, too. I get that from my mum. So you going to take
me on, then? You want to help me with my career?

GALE Well, I'd be – I'd like to get to know you a little bit better
first. How old are you, to start with, if you don't mind me
asking?

ROZ Sixteen. But they tell me I come over as much more mature.
I just been simply brilliant in *The Seagull*. Everybody said
I was. Everyone who came to see it. My mum, she was
crying at the end. Crying her head off. And she never cries,

my mum. My arsehole dad, before he left, he used to slap her senseless every weekend but I never saw her cry, never once. Don't give the bugger the satisfaction, she used to say. Anyway, he's left now. He's gone. Dead. Good riddance.

GALE Well. Men! Who needs them, eh?

ROZ Nah.

GALE So, how do you see your career developing from here? How do you see your future?

ROZ Well, fast as possible. Russ, my director, he's all for me going to drama school, getting, you know, training for two years, but I don't want to wait that long. I mean what's the point? I mean, you see people these days, they come straight off of the street some of them, ordinary people, never had no training in their lives, have they? And then all of a sudden they're stars, aren't they? One day they're, like, nobody and then all of a sudden they're someone. I don't want to waste time with training. I haven't got time for that. I just want to be there, you know. Up there, on top. Where I belong. I know I belong there. That's my plan, anyway.

ROZ, *now fully fired up, pauses for breath.* GALE *gapes at her.*

GALE Wow! It isn't every day I meet someone as confident as you.

ROZ *(smiling, unaware of any irony)* I bet you don't. So tell me about you. Have you got any – like – famous people on your books, have you?

GALE Oh, yes. One or two.

ROZ Who? Like who, for instance?

GALE Ah. Now. A large part of my job, Roz, an agent's job is very much to do with discretion. There has to be a bond of trust between the client and myself, you see? I'll just say this. Any time you go to a movie or you sit and watch a popular TV programme, at the top of the cast list you're very likely to see several of my clients' names above the title. Be assured, you'll be in good company, darling.

ROZ Fantastic.

From the other end of the room, the sound of voices and the piano as the others return from their break.

GALE Oughtn't you to be getting back to your rehearsal? They seem to be starting again.

ROZ Oh, yeah, right.

GALE Here, I'll give you my card. Drop into my office, we can chat some more. *(Producing her business card)* Call me first, though. I'm currently in the midst of changing addresses.

ROZ *(reading)* Force Ten Promotions. Gale Devonne.

RUSS *(offstage)* Roz! Are you coming back to join us, please?

GALE *(seeing* RUSS *for the first time)* Who's that?

ROZ That's Russ. My director.

GALE *(faintly)* Oh, my God! Russell! That's Russ.

ROZ Why, you know him then, do you?

GALE Ever so slightly, yes.

RUSS *re-appears.*

RUSS Now, Roz, provided you're prepared to enter into the spirit of things, Mrs Miller has agreed she's – *(He breaks off as he notices* GALE*)* Oh, I do beg your pardon, I didn't... *(Recognising her)* Gale? *(Incredulously)* Is it Gale?

GALE Hallo, Russell.

RUSS Oh, dear God! Gale! It is! Gale? How wonderful! How simply wonderful! We're just – we're just in the middle of – you've met Roz, of course?

GALE Yes, we've just been chatting...

RUSS Gale, what on earth are you doing here?

GALE *(with a glance at* ROZ, *hesitantly)* Well, I was...just...

RUSS What?

ROZ *(taking the hint)* Yes. I'll get back to rehearsals, then...

RUSS Yes, you'd better do that, Roz. And do please <u>try</u>... Please!

ROZ *(as she goes)* Yeah, yeah, yeah...

> ROZ *goes.*

RUSS *(to* GALE) Some minor artistic differences between her and our choreographer. Temporarily sorted. I hope. My God! That girl, sometimes... Such talent, too.

GALE Yes, so she was telling me.

RUSS Raw, you know but... No, tell me, what brings you here, Gale? What are you doing here?

GALE I'm only back here briefly. I just wanted to say a quick hallo, that's all. I was in the area, so I couldn't not...

RUSS Tell me, what are you doing these days? I followed your acting career but after a year or two I'm afraid I rather lost track of you...

GALE Yes, I'm afraid I did rather...lost touch...

RUSS What happened? I assumed you must have gone off to America or somewhere. To Hollywood perhaps...

GALE I wish. No, I've given it all up.

RUSS Given it up?

GALE Or rather I think it gave me up. No, nowadays, I've branched out on my own. I've started my own agency.

RUSS Really? An agency? For actors?

GALE For – performers.

RUSS Performers? Singers, dancers, you mean? That sort of thing?

GALE That sort of thing, yes.

RUSS How exciting!

GALE I've only just started.

A pause.

It's good to see you again, too. You haven't changed. Hardly.

RUSS Nor have you.

GALE Well, thanks for saying so, anyway.

RUSS No, I mean it. Not a jot, you haven't. *(Pause)* I'm a vicar. I never tell lies.

GALE *(smiling)* Oh, no?

A pause.

RUSS I've kept all your letters. You know, the ones you wrote – straight afterwards – early on.

GALE Did you? How sweet.

RUSS Did you keep mine? To you?

GALE No.

RUSS Ah.

GALE I kept them for a time. And then I thought, what's the point really? No, I mean, really? What was the point? We were never likely to see each other again. I was whisked away abroad. And if I'd ever set foot anywhere near you, your father would probably have set the dogs on me.

RUSS Nonsense. He wasn't like that. Not at all.

GALE He wrote to me, you know. Your father, the bishop. Telling me to stay well clear.

RUSS I don't believe that. Father would never –

GALE Russell, you have no idea what your father was capable of. It was a terrible letter, it really was. Couched in all the best Old Testament language. Virtually calling me a harlot. A cheap Jezebel seducing his beloved son... It's true, Russell. I'd show it you only I burnt that as well.

RUSS I had no idea he'd done that. Why would he do that?

GALE To protect you. Presumably. Misguidedly. He must have loved you very much.

RUSS Well, that's all changed, anyway. No love lost between us now. We haven't spoken a word to each other in over a year.

GALE Why's that?

RUSS I don't think he approves of the – path my career has taken. I think he had plans for me becoming a high flying career cleric...

GALE Like him?

RUSS More or less.

GALE I think that's one of the reasons I started writing to you. Because your father forbade me to.

RUSS And why did you stop writing?

GALE I said.

RUSS I kept writing to you for ages. Never heard a word back. I wasn't sure you were even getting them...

GALE Oh, I got them.

RUSS But you never replied?

GALE I've said, I couldn't see the point. Besides we'd rather run out of things to say to each other, hadn't we? Once I'd lost the baby, it was like the bond was broken... School kids' romance really, wasn't it? Time to grow up and move on.

RUSS If you'd kept the baby, would it have made a difference?

GALE Oh, come on, Russell. I was sixteen years old. The same age as that kid there. My whole life ahead of me... Finished my education at another distant school. Did OK. Scholarship to university... Got involved with the theatre crowd at Oxford, you know. Which put paid to my studies. I got sucked in to all that again. In the end, I decided theatre was much more fun and I simply quit. Went to drama school proper. Then out in the big wide world where I met the real competition. Suddenly everything came to a big full stop.

RUSS I see. So now you're an agent?

GALE Recently set up on my own. Well, don't sound so disappointed. There's nothing wrong with being an agent, you know.

RUSS No, I'm sorry. No. I mean, it's equally important that type of job, isn't it? Helping others?

GALE I think it is.

RUSS Are you doing well? Do you – do you – represent anyone famous? Anyone I may have heard of?

GALE Well, I'm still fairly new on the scene. But the books are overflowing with fresh talent. You would not believe the exciting young prospects there are around at present.

RUSS How wonderful. There's something deeply satisfying, isn't there, about finding youngsters, setting them up, helping them to realise their dreams? I mean, in my case they're usually disaffected, desperate kids, with no future to speak of, most of them destined for the social scrap heap. But sometimes, just occasionally, I find I can make a difference. I'll tell you something, do you know where I choose to take refuge these days? You'd think I'd choose the church, wouldn't you, as a sanctuary? But it's not. It's here in our community centre. This dilapidated old church hall of ours. This is where I tend to find peace, these days. Working with those kids. There's still a gleam of hope here, you see – those kids are still young enough, most of them, even the most deprived, to have some scrap of a dream left in them. And between us, together, we create fresh dreams. Try and make them flesh. In this dreary, under-heated, bleak place, its damp walls. The obscene graffiti. The appalling smell of drains you can never quite get rid of. The boarded up windows... Together here we create make believe. I mean, some of it's disastrous. Appalling. I look back on our Pirandello with sheer horror and as for our *Tempest*... I still get sleepless nights. But just occasionally – we do find the light – Now, our production of *The Seagull* – with Chekhov we soared – really got the air under our wings. I mean, I know most of the time I demand too much of them – far too ambitious. But as I keep saying to them, if we can't even try reaching for the sky, kids – how the hell can any of us ever hope to fly?

GALE *(smiling)* No wonder the kids love you. Do you get good audiences for your shows?

RUSS Not usually. We tend to be rather highbrow, I'm afraid. For local tastes. The occasional parent. Or proud grandparent. Even supposing they're remotely interested in their kids. In this area, generally not as a rule. Not a huge take up for Chekhov, not around these parts.

GALE Perhaps you should try something more popular?

RUSS *(wearily)* Oh, dear God, please, don't you start!

GALE Sorry. You know what they say about theatre? For every heart it lifts to heaven, it leaves ten broken in the gutter. Certainly did that to us, didn't it, when we were sixteen? Broke both our hearts –

RUSS Well, that was hardly the theatre's fault now, was it?

GALE No, it was that stupid school we were at. What were they thinking of? *Romeo and Juliet* with a load of over-sexed teenagers? Semi-nude bedroom scenes? What on earth did they expect?

RUSS Our onstage kiss got longer and longer every night, remember?

GALE That wasn't the only thing that did.

RUSS Sorry? What? Oh, I see. *(Very embarrassed)* You noticed that. I hoped you hadn't noticed.

GALE Couldn't help noticing, darling, there was hardly room in that bed for the three of us. Thank God we only did four performances or we'd have all been out on the balcony. There wouldn't have been room left in the bed.

RUSS *(laughing, anxious to change the subject)* Yes, anyway...

GALE Old Bill Pearson standing there in the wings hissing at us, 'Gale! Russell! Get on with it! Get a move on!'

RUSS Remember, after that final performance, the party, both of us sneaking away, over the playing fields – into Ten Acre Wood – lying under those pine trees –

GALE I was terrified I was going to get a fir cone wedged up my arse, you know.

RUSS – and we made love properly for the very first time – the full moon shining through the trees...

GALE New moon.

RUSS New moon? Are you sure?

GALE I was the one on my back.

RUSS It was an enchanted time, though, wasn't it? That was my first, did you know that? The very first time I ...you know...?

GALE Yes, I sort of guessed.

RUSS You guessed? How did you guess?

GALE Well, you did have a bit of trouble finding things, you know.

RUSS Did I? I don't remember that. Oh, God! Was that off-putting for you? Did you find that off-putting? You must have done.

GALE No, not really. It was sweet. Quite funny really. You were so serious about it. You kept saying, "Just a second. Nearly there. Sorry. Hang on! Just a tick!"

RUSS Oh, this is terrible. I'm so sorry. Now, I'm blushing, Gale... you're making me blush. Sorry.

GALE *(gently)* No, there's no need to be sorry. It was your first time.

RUSS It was for you too, wasn't it? The first time?

GALE *(lightly)* Oh, yes.

RUSS You told me then it was the first time for you, too.

GALE Oh, it was. Definitely. *(Sensing his doubt)* No, definitely. *(Slight pause)* Oh, Russell, really! What's it matter? First? Second? Third? Who knows?

RUSS Third? It can't have been your third, surely?

GALE Second, then.

RUSS Who was the first?

GALE It doesn't matter...

RUSS No, who? Please tell me! Who?

GALE Oh, really! What the hell does it matter now?

He waits.

Mr Kennedy.

RUSS Mr Kennedy? Mr Kennedy who taught us maths? That one? Oh, that's terrible. He was an appalling man. Why him of all people?

GALE He – he promised to give me a decent pass mark on my algebra paper.

RUSS *(appalled)* You let him – with you – for a pass mark in algebra? Gale, that's dreadful! It's quite shocking!

GALE Well, there was no other way I was going to pass algebra, was there? Then, of course, he reneged on our deal. Failed me anyway, the bastard.

RUSS Oh, this is dreadful.

GALE It was. Got my own back, though. Wrote an anonymous letter to his wife. Got him the sack eventually.

RUSS So that's why he left in the middle of term. I always wondered...

GALE What about you, then? You haven't told me about you, have you?

RUSS Oh, far less exciting than you. Far less. Finished school. Went on to uni to read English. And theology. Got a good result in English. Did a spot of teaching. Then, in the middle of it all, I suddenly felt, why resist the inevitable, so I went into the church.

GALE Was that pressure from your father?

RUSS Oh, slightly more than that. No, it was a genuine decision. I just felt I... I was already a believer, you know. I was always quite religious, thanks to Mother. Even at school. If you recall –

GALE When you weren't fumbling around in pine forests –

RUSS I always used to pray, you know. Practically the only one who did in my year. I got into the habit of it ever since I was tiny, praying with my mother before she – before we lost her. And then all alone at school in the dormitory – there were all these jokes, you know, at my expense. Drawing pins by the bed where I used to kneel. That sort of thing. But I soldiered on. Took it as some sort of Christian challenge, you know.

GALE What did you pray for?

RUSS Well, most of the time, once I got through the God bless Mummy, Daddy, Auntie Joan stage – later on, when I reached...pube – adulthood, I used to pray for someone like you to come along, really. Someone who'd come into my life and...and then when you did and we finally – got together, you know, I thought my prayers had been answered. And at that point I knew, you see, I knew for sure God existed somewhere – I knew for certain He did –

GALE *(amused)* Oh, Russell...

RUSS And then when we were both separated when you were whisked away by your parents, I thought, this is sent to test me – this is definitely sent to test my faith – and, you know, I've been praying ever since. That you'd come back. And now here you are. A second miracle!

GALE Russell – listen...

RUSS I'm never going to let you go again, Gale. I'm not going to let anyone take you away, ever again. We're back together, that's what matters now. This was meant, this was intended, all along. I know it was.

GALE *(gently but firmly)* Russell, listen to me! Listen! I have not come back for good, darling... I have my life now, Russell, my own quite separate, different life. In the same way that you have your life. I'm a very different person now, darling. To the one you used to know. If you knew me now, Russell, I doubt you would even like me very much...

RUSS Oh, that's nonsense. Don't you see, my life has been empty, waiting for you to walk back into it again. That's what I'm saying –

GALE *(slightly irritably now)* No, I haven't walked back into it, don't you understand? I simply came to...to say a brief hallo and goodbye. That's all this is.

RUSS *(bemused)* You're not staying, then?

GALE No.

RUSS *(agitated)* And all we went through meant nothing to you? After all we went through, together?

GALE *(exasperated, equally loudly)* Russell, what the hell are you talking about? It was bit of rough, clumsy, teenage sex, for God's sake!

They both look guiltily towards the rehearsal. It is suddenly rather quiet out there.

Oh, no, that's going to be all over the internet, isn't it? Look. Half of them have got their mobiles out already. Tweeting away! *(More confidentially)* It was just a bit of first time sex, Russell, that's all it amounted to. Most people forget all about that sort of thing. They move on.

RUSS Have you forgotten all about it?

GALE *(irritably)* I had till you bloody well reminded me! *(Pause)* No, of course I remember it. I remember every fucking detail. How could I forget something like that from which I – nearly produced a child as a result. But it was years ago. It's a part of my life I don't want to remember. If you must know, it makes me want to cry to think about it – to cry for what I was. For what I used to be.

RUSS *has crumpled. He sits miserably.*

Listen, this sounds rather pathetic now...but you couldn't possibly lend me some money, could you?

RUSS *(dead)* Money?

GALE I've – er – I've got quite a lot of financial problems at the moment and I badly need a loan to tide me over. Starting this new business – early days – and everything. I think I may have overstretched my resources...

RUSS You want me to lend you money...?

GALE I promise to pay it back. I wouldn't ask you if it wasn't rather desperate.

RUSS How much do you need?

GALE Well, in total, I'm looking for ten thousand –

RUSS *(stunned)* Pounds? Ten thousand pounds?

GALE Yes, I know it seems rather a lot but if you break it down –

RUSS I don't have ten thousand pounds, Gale! Ten thousand pounds?

GALE Yes, well, I know you personally don't... But I just thought your family...your father might possibly... I was just so desperate I'd never...no, no, forget it...you've said, you're not even on speaking terms with him...and once he knew it was for me... No, forget it. Mad. Forget I mentioned it. Sorry. Forget it!

RUSS *(shattered)* Is that why you came to see me? Just to borrow money?

GALE No, of course not! Of course I didn't! No!

RUSS I see...

A commotion from the other end of the room.

MRS M (*furiously, offstage*) No, no, no, no, NO! You stupid girl! You're stupid, do you hear me? You're stupid, stupid, stu – (*A cry of pain*) Aah!

Her voice cuts off abruptly.

The sound of excited cheering.

RUSS *and* **GALE** *look towards the source of the commotion.*

RUSS (*moving towards the commotion*) Oh, no! Dear heaven! What on earth's the girl done now...?

ROZ *comes storming on.*

ROZ (*as she appears*) I warned her, I warned her, didn't I...?

RUSS Roz, what have you done? What on earth made you do that?

ROZ (*heading for the door*) I'm going home!

RUSS Roz, if you walk out now, I'm warning you –

ROZ (*angrily*) I'm not discussing it no more. If you want to discuss it, you talk to my fucking agent!

ROZ *goes out.*

RUSS (*bemused*) Your agent? Who on earth's your agent...?

GALE *shrugs, as if denying all knowledge.*

Oh, God! (*Making to follow* **ROZ**) Roz? Roz! Come back...

Before he can go off, **MRS MILLER**, *the choreographer, middle-aged and slightly overweight, hurries on. A blood soaked tissue clasped to her face.*

Mrs Miller...!

MRS M *(muffled, distressed)* She's broken my nose! The wretched girl's broken my nose!

RUSS Mrs Miller, let me see... Let me see!

MRS MILLER *shrugs him away.*

She pauses to collect her coat from the pile on the sofa.

MRS M *(muffled)* That girl is homicidal! She should be locked up!

RUSS Mrs Miller –

MRS M *(hurrying off)* I need an ambulance! Call an ambulance!

MRS MILLER *goes out towards the front door.* RUSS *follows her.*

RUSS *(as he goes, calling back)* It's alright, Stan – Mr Rattenbury, I'm dealing with this!

After a second, sounds of the rehearsal restarting. Having abandoned the dance sequence, they are apparently preparing to run through a song. GALE *watches.*

GALE *(to herself, quite impressed)* My, God! What have I taken on there?

RUSS *comes hurrying back through.*

RUSS *(as he enters, calling)* First aid box! Would someone please locate the first aid box, which for the tenth time is not in the place it should be! *(To* GALE *as he goes)* Gale, wait there please! I must talk to you!

RUSS *goes off to the rehearsal area.*

GALE *hesitates for a moment. She swiftly comes to a decision.*

GALE *(making a decision)* No, no, no... Enough said!

GALE *exits swiftly to the front door.*

RUSS *returns with a first aid box.*

He stops, noticing GALE *has gone.*

RUSS Gale? Gale? She can't have gone, surely? ...Not just like that... Gale!

He hurries out towards the front door.

Offstage, the piano strikes up the introduction to **"THREE LITTLE MAIDS".**

(re-entering, crestfallen) Oh, God, what a terrible day!

Offstage, two girls start singing **"THREE LITTLE MAIDS"**, *altering it to 'two little maids'.*

RUSS, *despite himself, dutifully stands nodding, conducting and making encouraging gestures to them.*

That's good! That's lovely, girls! Splendid. Plenty of energy, Tracy, energy now! Look as if you're enjoying it, dear. It's fun, remember! Fun! Have fun! Fun...

He finally cannot keep up the pretence any longer. He turns away from them and starts to cry, his sobs grow louder, but fortunately for him are drowned out by Sullivan's exuberant music.

The lights fade to: –.

Blackout.

PROPS

THE AGENT
Mobile phone
Sofa
Coffee table
Armchair
Desk with a phone
Swivel chair
Two upright chairs
A table near the window
Phone and landline cable
Black hair tie

THE JUDGE
A desk with a swivel chair. On the desk, a framed, fifty-year-old photograph of an attractive young woman in her twenties
Sofa with cushions and a coffee table plus an easy chair
A table with a white cloth, laid up for dinner for two and two dining chairs
TV remote control
Champagne glasses
Ice bucket
Half-empty tin of assorted biscuits on a tray
Tray with two mugs of cocoa
Champagne bottle
Phone on desk
Walking stick
Dining trolley with two soup bowls, covered tureen and ladle, bread rolls

THE NOVELIST
Various receptacles are dotted about the room to catch the drips from the leaking roof, including a three-quarter filled bucket
A bell – a remote radio unit
Book
Sofa

Coffee table
Armchair
Desk
Desk chair
Table and two upright chairs
Walking stick
Watch

THE POLITICIAN
Desk with a swivel chair
A table alongside piled with files and other paperwork
A sofa with coffee table and an easy chair make an informal
area
Upright chair x2
Handbag
Mobile phone x2
Watch
Coat
Brown envelope
Ghetto blaster

THE STAR
A table and two chairs
A sofa untidily piled with the coats and outerwear
An inverted armchair and a coffee table both evidently long
unfit for purpose
Desk with a swivel chair, apparently the dumping centre for
schoolbags
Script
A blood soaked tissue
First Aid box
Business Card

LIGHTING

THE AGENT
The lights fade to Blackout (p24)

THE JUDGE
Adjusts to the lighting level via a dimmer switch so the room gets slightly darker (p33)
Blackout (p52)

THE NOVELIST
Through the glass, a flash of lightning (p65)
Lights fade to blackout (p76)

THE POLITICIAN
Lights fade to blackout (p101)

THE STAR
Lights fade to blackout (p127)

SOUND EFFECTS

THE AGENT
Front door buzzer sounds (p1)
Buzzer sounds again (p2)
Flat's doorbell rings (p2)
Heavy knocking on the front door (p2)
More heavy knocking (p2)
More knocking (p2)
Loud thud and crash as the front door is splintered off and falls to the hall floor (offstage) (p3)
The sound of distant traffic (p7)

THE JUDGE

TV set drones on (p27)
Kills unseen TV sound (p29)
Phone on the desk rings (p29)
The doorbell chimes (p33)

THE NOVELIST

We hear the drips occasionally throughout (p55)
Tapping on outer door (p55)
Further knocking (p55)
A rumble of thunder (p62)
A bell inside the desk rings loudly (p63)
The bell rings again, continuously this time (p63)
Bell still ringing, louder now (p64)
Bell stops (p64)
A loud rumble of thunder (p66)
More thunder (p69)
Another clap of thunder (p72)
Another rumble of thunder (p75)
The bell machine – sound it makes begins to resemble the high pitched underwater scream of a woman's voice (p76)

THE POLITICIAN

Intercom on his desk buzzes (p80)
Mobile phone rings (p81)
The bell to the outer office door rings (p83)
The front door bell rings again (p84)
The doorbell rings again (p84)
The doorbell rings again (p85)
Mobile phone rings (p87)
Mobile phone rings (p88)
She switches off her phone with a beep (p88)
From outside the sound of raised voices (p92)
A drum and bass track cuts in at volume: She sets her ghetto blaster off.
A loud chord to start her off. (p98)
Phone chimes as a message comes through (p98)
Backing tape stops (p98)
A distant door slams (p99)
Music fades (p101)

THE STAR

The piano stops abruptly – various young voices raised in protest and dissent (p105)

Offstage rehearsal activity including dance number, piano accompaniment and occasional interruptions (p105)

Offstage rehearsals appear to have stopped temporarily.

A murmur of voices (p109)The sound of voices and the piano (p114)

It is suddenly rather quiet out there (p123)

A commotion from the other end of the room (p125)

The sound of excited cheering (p125)

Sounds of the rehearsal restarting (p126)

Two girls start singing "THREE LITTLE MAIDS", altering it to 'two little maids' (p127)

Piano strikes up the introduction to "THREE LITTLE MAIDS" (127)

VISIT THE SAMUEL FRENCH BOOKSHOP AT THE ROYAL COURT THEATRE

Browse plays and theatre books, get expert advice and enjoy a coffee

Samuel French Bookshop
Royal Court Theatre
Sloane Square
London
SW1W 8AS
020 7565 5024

Shop from thousands of titles on our website

 samuelfrench.co.uk

 samuelfrenchltd

 samuel french uk